The Voice Across the Veil

Powerful Messages from Beyond that Give Us All Hope...

Sue Scudder

Copyright 2010 Susan D. Scudder

First Edition: ISBN 0-9845417-0-5 United States of America
Second Edition ISBN: 1530283353

All rights reserved. No part of this book may be reproduced or transmitted in any form or by any means, electronic or mechanical, including photocopying, recording, or by any information storage and retrieval system, without permission in writing from the copyright owner.

Contact Information:
Email: sue.scudder@gmail.com
Websites: www.SueScudder.com

Cover Design: Sue Scudder
Photography & Artwork by Sophia Rose

Editors: Trice Hufnagel & Claire Pearson

Facilitation: Kim Savage, EMDR Specialist

Consultation: Barbara Snow

The Voice Across the Veil

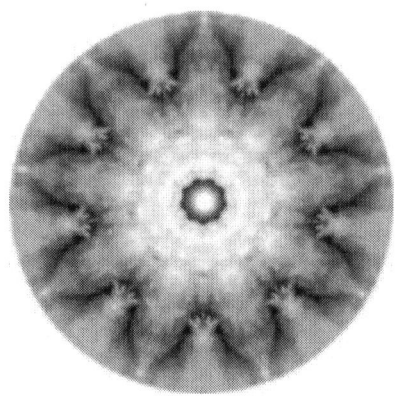

Cover photo

artwork and

photography by

Sophia Rose

This book is dedicated to:

My husband and best friend.
Thanks for being all that you are.
I will love you forever.

My dearest daughter.
You have touched my heart deeply
by being the beautiful person you are.
Thanks for your complete understanding
and for choosing us as your parents.
I love you so much!

Namaste

*I honor the place within you
where the entire Universe resides.
I honor the place within you
of love and light,
of peace and truth.
I honor the place within you where,
when you are in that place in you
and I am in that place in me,
there is only one of us.*

Contents

Acknowledgements 12
Preface 15

PART I

1. Life on Both Sides 23
2. The Voice Across the Veil 31
3. Seven Divine Spirits of Light 37
4. Sisters of the Moon 43
5. Communicating Between Worlds 49
6. Drafted for Spiritual Work 61
7. A Dream Relived 73
8. The Past Reawakened 79
9. Released from the Past 87

PART II

10. Sacred Friends 101
11. All Embracing Love............................109
12. Ethereal Messages.............................121
13. Walk Gently on the Earth 137
14. Our Endless Life 151

Epilogue 161

Glossary..164
About the Author 170
Author's Note 172
About the Artist 175

Acknowledgements

To all of my family and lifelong friends, old and new: I am blessed to share my path with all of you. With gratitude and respect I honor my teachers and guides, seen and unseen, who have encouraged me every step of the way to bring forth this illuminated, loving information shared with me by those phenomenal souls who have walked on this earth and blessed us with their experiences.

Special thanks and honor to my spirit sisters, Doris, Angie and Althea, with much love.

With great admiration, respect and love to my dear friend Jane for all that you are.

In honor and love to E.M.E.K. and her circle of loved ones.

With appreciation and love I thank Alan and Faye for exploring our "trek" together. With respect I thank Weston Jolly for assisting me in finding my purpose.

I am thankful for my gifted photographer and artist, Sophia Rose, whose brilliance brings beautiful energy and light through her artwork.

Trice, thank you with much love, for your help and support – you touch the lives of many.

In honor and gratitude to Ruby for your earth-centered teaching.

I am grateful for my sweet editor, Claire Pearson, who guided me along the way.

Special thanks and love to Jayne for your integral contribution to our experience.

Thanks to the lovely, incredible women in my life who have supported and encouraged me – Allyn, Doris, Rayah Donna, and Barbara– you are special lights in my life.

The names of all the dear ones in this book, who touched me deeply, have been changed out of respect for them and their loved ones. You know who you are. Thank you for being in my life.

In this time of spiritual growth, I honor Spirit, Source of All Things, as each of us individually perceives love.

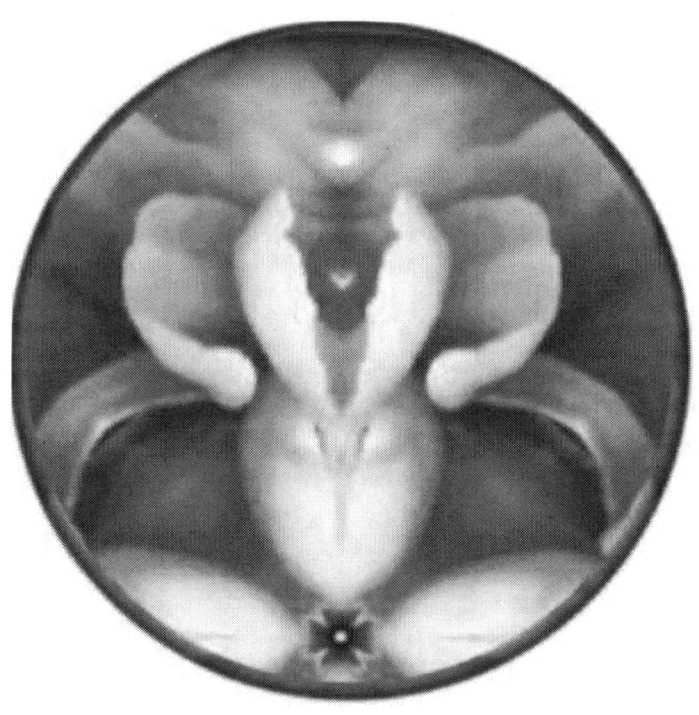

Preface

Music is the connecting thread that brings lovely people into my life, music divinely guided. In the Rocky Mountains west of Denver, Colorado, I write original compositions for piano and accompanying orchestration. I am a musician.

The true events of my life in this book are the deepest notes of my life song. I now play them for you, the thread that binds us all. Because no matter who we are, we all have access to the Creator that resides within.

This book is my experience. May this writing, inspired from my life and soul memories, touch you with divine fulfillment from the spark of life within us all.

Sue Scudder

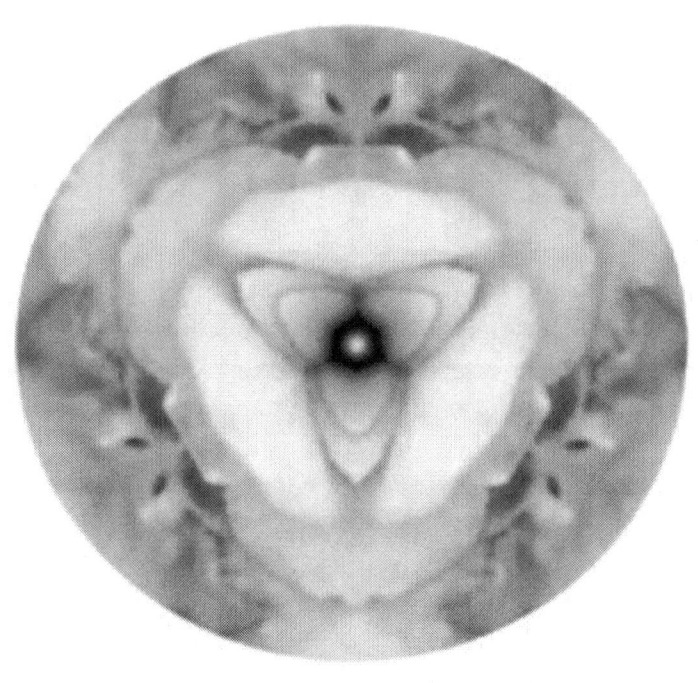

"In all actuality,
we are eternal beings
traveling on this planet
in human bodies."

Sue Scudder

Part I

"Be love,

create love

and love all

things"

Life on Both Sides

Life on Both Sides

Mother's Day, May 1988, four months after giving birth to my daughter, I was wheeled down a hospital hall for emergency surgery to treat a ruptured appendix.

I had never experienced general anesthesia before and felt a premonition that this was not going to be a routine operation. The nurse peered down over my head, a mask covering her nose and mouth. The upside-down view of her long, overdone eyelashes and the thick black eyeliner surrounding each eye was etched in my mind.

"You seem nervous," she said. "Are you worried?"

I nodded.

"This is a common procedure," she attempted to comfort me. "Everything will be fine."

That was all I remembered until sometime later I heard, "Code Blue! Code Blue!" over the intercom and saw two male hospital aides run out of the operating room doors at top speed. My husband and sister-in-law looked at each other in shock – *I* was in that operating room.

At first I didn't realize I was floating above my body. I thought I was dreaming as I witnessed the reactions to this emergency – my emergency – from the ceiling of the waiting room.

I was floating in a peaceful, serene, radiant light and felt quite natural. Then in the velvety-smooth brilliance, I floated beyond this world. It was a *familiar* feeling – like something you know you have experienced but can't quite place.

I found myself in a majestic realm, standing in front of a shining, ornate gate. When it opened, I walked into golden-white light. In the illuminated space, I came upon two large sandstone-colored doors with pillars on either side . . . and felt very safe, cared for and loved. I entered and peered around a large expansive column. "Where am I?" I thought, walking alone through a building reminiscent of a library. Everything appeared to be made of light-colored marble and I noticed that there were no shadows.

I walked through a maze of enormous white rooms, discovering a large marble bench and pulpit. I looked up. Seven divine spirits of light, immersed in incandescent splendor, looked down upon me and smiled warmly. Their complete and total love embraced me. Noticing I was overwhelmed, they laughed tenderly and asked me to sit on the bench across from them. In the immensity of the room, I felt like a child. I later realized that they were part of the Council of Twelve.

The seven divine spirits of light described to me my life destiny and the path I had chosen for myself long ago. I found myself recalling the plan . . . and I now *knew* it had to do with my music.

"You will have spiritual guidance and help," they said.

"Yes!" I answered enthusiastically. "And I *can* do it if I will have your help."

"You won't remember much of this conversation," they said, "until it is time to fulfill your destiny."

I never forgot that meeting, or the very meaningful conversation with those ethereal beings, although the depth of the content did escape me.

"She's waking up!" I clearly heard. I knew I was in the recovery room, even though I wasn't completely back from my trip.

A nurse said, "Susan, I don't want you to be alarmed, but you are completely paralyzed."

"*What!*"

That woke me up! I tried to move. I couldn't even open my eyes. The nurse explained that I had an allergic reaction to the anesthesia, and it would wear off in about ten hours. I was on a respirator – the only way I could breathe.

The Voice Across the Veil

I was terrified! I was *so* aware of everything around me, yet couldn't move a muscle. My senses were exceptionally clear, even though I was trapped in a physical body. Was this what people experience in a coma? I wondered. Helpless entrapment?

Although I couldn't speak or move, I heard every word spoken around me by the caregivers and my loved ones who visited. I may have looked oblivious, but I was *present*.

Later, another nurse said, "Let's see if she can breathe on her own yet." Terror struck me because I was completely helpless. I had no way of conveying to them that the respirator was still doing the actual breathing for me.

In my mind I screamed, "*No! Don't turn it off. I still need it!*"

The machine stopped and I stopped breathing. They turned it back on immediately. I tried to sleep, to be unconscious and out of my frozen form. I came in and out for a while. After several hours, I could move my eyelids and then communicate by blinking my eyes in answer to questions. Then I could wiggle my toes. It was another five hours before I began to regain control of my physical body. I didn't go home for another three weeks and dearly missed my beautiful new baby, Heather, and my endearing husband, Stephen. Later, I told him about my "dream" of hearing the code-blue warning and seeing the aides running out of the operating room.

Stephen looked startled.

"How did you know that was happening?"

"I was floating just above you. I saw everything that happened!"

After my memorable out-of-body adventure I had a new appreciation for life . . . and a new understanding: we as humans and the spirit world are very closely connected. I had gone from a physical being to a spiritual being, and back again, in twenty-four hours, coming out more integrated on *both* sides of life. I was the same person. Here *and* there, I was still *me*. Who I was never changed in either form.

Follow your
dreams,
follow your
heart."

The Voice Across the Veil

The Voice Across the Veil

My hospital experience awakened an insatiable curiosity to learn as much as I could about the other side of life and all things mystical. I began to forge a strong connection with my spirit guides and personal angels.

I was very fortunate to have many wonderful teachers and mentors to guide my learning, some of whom touched on my ethereal experience but could get no more information than what I remembered. I only came to understand the levels of connections possible twelve years later, when I met Jonathan Westley, a spiritual channel from Sedona, Arizona. Jonathan set aside his personality to allow nonphysical beings to speak through him, providing incredible information that only his clients would know.

A small weekend seminar in June 2000, provided the backdrop for my first encounter with Jonathan. All the trees and flowers were in bloom on this warm Friday evening in Denver, Colorado. I drove to my destination through landscaped medians covered with vivid yellow daffodils, purple pansies and red tulips.

Upon arrival I found my friend Martha, who had invited me. Only four other people were in the audience with us. Jonathan Westley, the speaker, had just published his first book and was not yet widely known.

I had no idea what to expect from this handsome, tall man, whose sandy-brown hair and blue eyes disguised his forty-five years. He introduced himself cheerfully and began explaining how and why he became a spiritual channel and advisor. Jonathan was bright, perky and always laughing. With his appealing sense of humor and zestful manner, his presentation was truly captivating.

He explained that he was born with this gift but only now, after an awakening and with the support of his family, had he started to help others. He also explained that he allows many different spirits of light – nonphysical beings – to speak through him. Who comes through depends on the people for whom he is channeling. Jonathan also serves as a conduit, or medium, for deceased loved ones during private sittings and telephone sessions.

After his introduction, Jonathan sat on a stool positioned in front of us, closed his eyes and began to center. His voice slowed and softened. His expressions and demeanor changed. His arms and legs twitched as if the energy was too much for the body it was in; the lights hanging overhead started crackling and flashing. Although I instinctively knew the wisdom channeled was true, I was stunned – I had never before witnessed anything like this.

After the general messages from spirit, Jonathan accurately described the life of each person in attendance. I was astonished. He mentioned my brother, aspects of my childhood, and a great deal about my music. Then he looked straight at me and said, "The blood, the blood is everywhere!"

A chill ran through me.

"Does that mean anything to you?" he asked

"No. Not at all," I answered.

Saturday was filled with workshop exercises to help us learn and grow spiritually.

Later that day, Jonathan again mentioned my music.

A flash of the memory of my visit with the seven spirits filled my head. Was it finally time to start unraveling the puzzle of my destiny?

After that incredible weekend, I made an appointment with Jonathan for a private channeling session before he left Denver. We met on Sunday afternoon. First to come through was Catherine, the angel who has been with me since I was a child. Her voice and demeanor at all times were loving and kind. I always felt safe, nurtured and encouraged in her presence. This was a definite confirmation of truth and authentic guidance.

Catherine said, "Your path is intertwined with your music."

Even hearing that made me a little nervous. I didn't have much experience sharing my original compositions with the outside world. Would people want to hear my work? Would they even like it? All of a sudden the possible agreement I had made in the presence of the spirit beings became ominous.

"Do not fear child, it does not matter if it is words or musical notes or any other form of creation," Catherine stated, reading my mind. "If it is created in the light of truth, it is a bridge to brilliance that will touch the hearts of many."

It was at this point I decided to pursue creating my first CD, *Celebration of Light*.

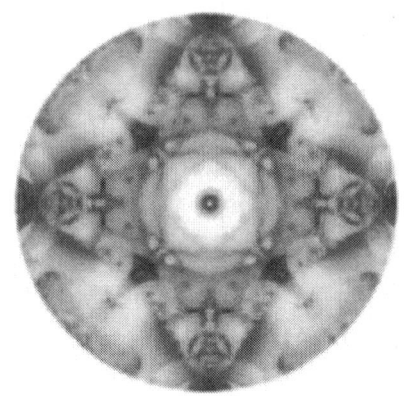

Seven Divine Spirits of Light

Seven Divine Spirits of Light

After my brush with death, my vision of the seven elders drifted through my mind on and off throughout my life. I tried so hard to remember the conversation – even having others with clairvoyant abilities try to get a glimpse – but to no avail.

I could still remember the out of body experience and the place as if it were yesterday. The seven elders were enormous, probably nine feet tall or more in our world. They dressed in what looked like white robes, but were perhaps light – in spirit form they had long white hair; some had long beards and eyes sparkling with kindness. The feeling these elders gave me is one I will never forget, nor can I describe it using human terms. Surrounded in brilliant golden-white light, they possessed unquestionable wisdom of the ages. I am completely humbled just at the thought of standing before them.

The realization of the message came back to me only now – nineteen years later. And when it did, I was once again standing in front of the gracious beings – having been led there by the angel whom I have worked with for many years.

This time walking along side my angel, Catherine, in meditation, I stood before the seven divine spirits of light and easily recalled the conversation as I transcribed it through automatic writing.

"Welcome, this is not your time to be here but we have much to say to you, dear one. You have a great future you haven't begun to embark upon. We know your fear of the music; but you must keep working with it as this is the thread that binds you to others.

It will play major importance in your life as it advances.

"Forget the past as it is not important now. You will meet many on your path that you will recognize from other times. They will help you grow. Not all will be of bliss but they will help you none the less – and you will help them.

"Your purpose is to help others cross from one side to another, as you are experiencing right now. You will explain in a great way to many living on your side that each of you are eternal spirits in human bodies in a physical world.

"You will struggle with this concept as you still want to be accepted in the human world. You will write a book for all to read, conducted by us. Your fear will well up. You will search for others to help. No one can. You must do this on your own. Your writing will be widely read and accepted as the truth it is. It must, however, have no influence from others on Earth that may want to alter your truth.

"There will be some resentment at first because you will be working with people who are well known through tragedy. This resentment will subside. The individuals you will work with will assist in bringing about the message. This is NOT a self-fulfilling journey as you will perceive it in a fearful way; rather, it is your purpose, your destiny. Again, your music will tie it all together.

"The first person to ask for your assistance will be a friend. The next person who needs your help will have experienced a great tragedy orchestrated long ago. A young girl, swept away, will touch the hearts of many.

"You must release all fear."

"Yes, I *can* and will if I have your help." I replied.

"You *have* our help. You will be helping us get messages across in this way!

"You will face frightening odds when you return, but it will not last long."

The Voice Across the Veil

My next vision was back in the recovery room. I again heard the nurse say "Susan, I don't want you to be alarmed - - - -"

As I came out of this meditation, I realized the reason for my memory loss. Had I known nineteen years ago that, as a result of painful tragedies, I would be assisting and communicating with "dead" people, what would the last nineteen years of my life have been like? Looking around every corner – what is the tragedy and who might it affect? Writing a book? I am not a writer! I would surely have lost my mind. It was a good and righteous thing to have had my memory erased for a time.

The reference to the music was scary enough for me. I experienced paralyzing performance anxiety as the result of childhood pressures and perceptions placed upon me by certain members of my family.

So I had passed through the last nineteen years learning and growing in many ways – becoming one with the music and also with the dance of life once again.

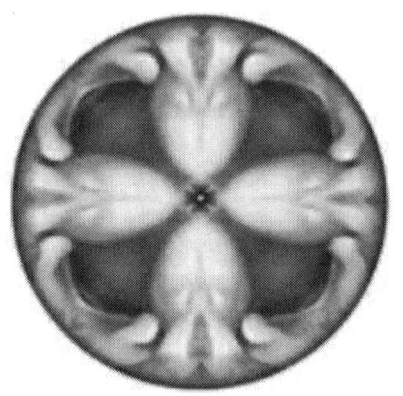

Sisters of the Moon

Sisters of the Moon

Sometimes people you encounter create life-changing experiences that you share and never forget. In 1998 my daughter, Heather, was taking horseback-riding lessons and learning to train Arabian show horses at a stable near our home.

Dory was taking English-riding lessons at the same time. I noticed her bright spirit right away and immediately felt a connection with her. On her petite, well-trained Arabian gelding, with her long, curly light-brown hair and slight build, Dory looked like a fairy floating along with the rhythm of the horse beneath her.

Inside the large, cold, windowless arena, heated only by a wood stove at the entrance, Dory approached me one afternoon and asked if I would be interested in forming a women's meditation group. The idea was to support and help each other grow spiritually and, through meditation, send loving energy into the universe to help heal our planet and humanity.

Fourteen women attended our first meeting where we waded through many agendas. As the months went on, the numbers dropped off down to a group of four: Dory, Rose, Ann, and myself.

Dory, an artist from New York, lived in Italy for a while, exploring her talent. She exudes creative passion, her blue eyes sparkling with imagination.

Rose is an enchanting person of illumination with a wonderful sense of humor. Tall, thin, and fair, with green eyes and a gigantic smile, she feels the interconnection of all things.

Ann, from the South, is a massage therapist. She is calm, serene and down to earth, also tall, with dark hair and deep brown eyes. She was the caretaker of our animals, affirming our oneness with nature and helping us strengthen our grounding with the earth.

One of my contributions to the group was my music, which we used for meditation. As Dory was such a talented artist, I was honored when she offered to design the cover of my first CD.

We were all different, yet focused on serving others. We were four 'old souls' with a huge glossary of teachings, born into this lifetime and brought together for a purpose. Initially we came together to learn how to better incorporate our spiritual nature into our everyday lives. We drew much strength from our Native American earth-centered spiritual teachings. By collectively combining all of our resources, we discovered an unexpected and incredible spiritual power.

We all lived in the foothills of the same Rocky Mountain community at 8,500 feet, so we took turns sharing our homes for the setting of our meetings in the majesty of the mountains. At our monthly full-moon meetings, we alternated sharing and leading our favorite meditation methods and guided imagery exercises. On many occasions we read excerpts from meaningful books and shared our teachings with each other. Much of our time was spent meditating together and sharing our thoughts and visions afterward.

We always invited the spirits of universal love to be present. At the end of each full-moon gathering, Dory, Rose, Ann, and I stood in a circle holding hands. We visualized a gold string emanating from our hearts, connecting us and joining at the center of the circle. We saw the golden-white light envelop us, then expand up and spread out into the world until it completely encompassed the planet.

With full devotion and peaceful intention, we sent that energy out to all people on the planet to heal the earth and to help disaster victims, to comfort those who were grieving, and those who were touched by war. We sent healing, harmony, and universal love to the animal kingdom, the plant kingdom and our friends and family. With our intention of highest good to all, we saw the light reach to the far corners of the earth and to all minds and hearts. Incredible love bloomed through us.

As we grew in confidence and knowledge of the significance of our meetings, we learned more about working with the ethereal realm beyond. We felt Spirit pouring light into our beings, which moved us to tears of sweetness. That *feeling* is the most beautiful affirmation of the masterful, angelic presence.

Everyone has the innate ability to meditate and connect with Source. Some people see with the mind's eye, some feel or sense, some just know, some hear. Some people rely on one gift more than the others; some use more than one of these extrasensory skills. We use them all the time subconsciously.

Communicating Between Worlds

Communicating Between Worlds

Little did we Sisters of the Moon realize the potential we were developing during our monthly full-moon gatherings, although we did suspect we were being guided to a higher purpose of service.

In the spring of 2001, during one of my telephone sessions with the spiritual channel, Jonathan Westley, something phenomenal happened. Many times the beings speaking through him merely referred to themselves as "we," unless I specifically asked their names. My angel, Catherine, came through often along with a number of other light beings as well.

The Voice Across the Veil

This day I was speaking to Catherine about my women's group and asked if we had a higher purpose. "What would you have us do to be of service?"

Angel Catherine said, "It is very important you allow others to come within the circle. These people need not to be real, as you would describe it in the physical form, yet they are very happy to step within to gain the assistance of the healing mothers. There is greatness in your choice to send them energy and encouragement as they continue their trek, their passage through this time."

"Are you talking about beings on the other side?" I asked.

"Yes, very much so. Some who have passed remain confused. They can use some help from your side of the fence."

"You mean helping people transition to the light?" I asked.

"Yes, especially those who have transcended quickly through sudden departure."

"Like my friend, Sam?"

"Yes. We are glad for you to speak of him for even now he needs assistance."

About two years prior, in April, 1999, my husband Stephen and I had lost a dear friend in an automobile accident. Sam was on his way to work one morning. When he was about five miles from his home driving toward town on the highway, two teenagers pulled out in front of him. A pickup truck was coming toward them from the opposite direction. So, to save their lives, Sam drove off the embankment – a thirty-foot drop. He died almost immediately. In life, he had been a Disaster Recovery Manager. He had thought of those young people first.

Sam, in his early forties, left behind his wife, Jennifer, and three daughters. What I remember most about Sam was his quick wit and wonderful sense of humor. He loved to make people laugh. He had a strong faith and took it very seriously. Known as a gentle man who always put his family first, his tragic death shook the entire community.

Jennifer and I had always been close friends. Music brought us together initially, as she is a very talented singer. I spent a lot of time arranging piano accompaniments for her beautiful voice and cherished her company – she is one of the sweetest people I know. I tried to help her, any way I could, by offering healing energy work and being there when she needed me.

"How can I help Sam?" I asked the angels.

"We are suggesting that he be placed in the center of love as you help him with his transition. Guiding him through the breath of light like a feather, allowing him to have free-will choice to glide to his beauty – to his highest state. We, the ones in the light, desire to receive him. We extend our hands and yet he continues to need encouragement."

"Is he having a difficult time leaving his wife and

children?" I questioned. Then, quite suddenly, the voice speaking through Jonathan changed.

"Yes, very much so," said the spirit. "It is good for me to go. I am very hopeful that you can help me on my path."

I took a deep, slow breath. "Is this Sam?"

"Yes."

I was shocked and astonished to be actually speaking to my deceased friend. The possibility of something like this happening never occurred to me. Not only that, he was asking for my help! Having no idea how to proceed, I carefully chose my next statement.

"Sam, you were the example of the way Spirit wants us to live on earth."

"Are you sure?' he said. "I have had many doubts, especially in leaving so many things undone. I always liked to do things well."

"It was painful," I replied. "It is very painful for Jennifer and the girls, but their strong faith is getting them through this. You can be proud of them."

"I am," Sam said. "And I continue to be very happy, but I miss my incarnate form and not being able to support them. It is frustrating to not be felt, sensed and known by them. This is why I have dragged my feet about moving on. My guides continually call me to the light, yet I have held back. I do not want to leave Jennifer completely alone. I feel very strongly about this. I do not want to cause any more pain to anyone. I need your help. This is what I have come to ask you and your group, hoping you will encourage me. I want to go in this way.

"I wish for you to participate with vibrations if this is your choice," Sam continued. "Do not be afraid to share your music. Maybe even take a tip or two." I knew right away that by vibrations Sam meant my music. He had always been one of my biggest supporters and he loved my piano compositions. He was encouraging me to embrace my music by his visual of using a tip jar as one would see placed on a piano during a casual performance.

"I am happy to find voice," he said. "It feels good to speak again – there are so many things to say. Being in this state is like having the privilege of walking, yet no longer having feet to take me where I want to go. It is difficult to converse with those on earth. The ones I affectionately call mine . . . *I do miss* them. I merely need their permission to go forward. Will you help? Will you *please* help? This is why I cry out. Catherine, the angel, so sweet, so beautiful, brought me here, knowing it would be okay to ask for your time. I do not mean to interfere."

"You don't ever have to apologize," I said.

"I don't mean to barge in," Sam said. "I have always been like this. I was a little hesitant, yet the angel, Catherine, said it is time. It is time to have conversation. I need the encouragement of your group to help me on my way. God is so divinely beautiful; I wanted all my life to return to the Source of my being, yet I pause here. I need to go. This is why I want your assistance – to set me free. I seek to be with God. I am called. I am happy to return. These are tears of joy, pure joy, as I remember the vibrations that draw me." I noticed Jonathan was actually crying as Sam spoke through him.

"Are you with us when I am doing energy work with Jennifer?" I asked.

"Yes, very much so."

"I will try to get messages to her if that is what you would like, although I don't want to upset Jennifer, as she may not embrace a lot of this."

"Yes, I know, yet she is so cute."

"She is lovely, Sam, and so strong. Your daughters are strong too. Your family will let you go; they want you to be in the light and want only the best for you. Your memory will never be lost."

"This is true. It is impossible to erase. That is not something that is understood by many of those on the physical side. Our existence in the incarnate form is never lost, though many build shrines to identify what has transcended. I do not need to be remembered in that way. I enjoyed my time on earth. I am pleased to go on. I so want to return Home. I want my family to know I will continue to be with them, yet it is important I finish my passing."

"Do you understand how loved you were here?" I

asked.

"Yes. I have felt it many times. I continue to feel the emotions of the circumstances and situations of my duration on earth. I also have viewed my imperfections, not that it is super important. I sought to do things according to a life plan that befit me."

"You touched the heart of everyone who crossed your path, Sam."

"Yes, I feel it, more real here than there. I didn't really comprehend then. It is so beautiful to understand this now. In meetings that take place afterwards, (I call them meetings because there is really no good word for the connection that occurs when one changes form) the feelings are so beautiful, so comfortable – like perfect nourishment coming from a woman's breast, knowing that the food has been divinely prepared. Knowing all that is coming through is exactly what the child – baby – is in need of. It is likened to this in the very majestic way, going beyond what the incarnate expressions are able to capture. I have used these pictures, words, and feelings as a means to best describe how it is here."

"What exactly can I do for you Sam?"

"Through the gathering of your intimate group, allow me to be invited, felt, and seen. This is important to me as I want to exist in this form, even in a translucent state, before exiting. Assistance in transcending and ceremony is part of the experience that you will share with the group.

It will be very powerful. It will be very strong. It is part of something that we have all agreed to participate in.

I felt intuitively that my sisters would all agree to help Sam, although I had no idea what to do or exactly how to fulfill this request. I would share his request with them as soon as possible.

"Others need assistance as well," Sam said. "I am pleased to be the first one to step into the center of your circle."

"The next full moon, Sam?"

"Yes. It will happen in a flash. It is merely my choice to remain hesitant. I do not wish to leave the hearts of those with whom I participated. I am constantly drawn to Jennifer and she is always on my mind. She has so much strength – so much beauty.

"It is important that your group gather quickly because I want to go. Not in the form of time, for I am not constrained in this way, but I do need to continue on my path."

"We will help you," I assured Sam.

"Thank you. This is also my means of helping others who need facilitation to transcend. It is difficult for them, not knowing they can have support on your side as well. Many here simply need encouragement to go to the light."

I confirmed Sam's request: "So you wish for us to invite you into our circle and give you the encouragement that you need?"

"Yes, and I thank you. I bow in honor to you. I honor you for your choice to continue facilitating others."

"I understand, Sam, and I will help with great love."

"The beautiful
light
is unending"

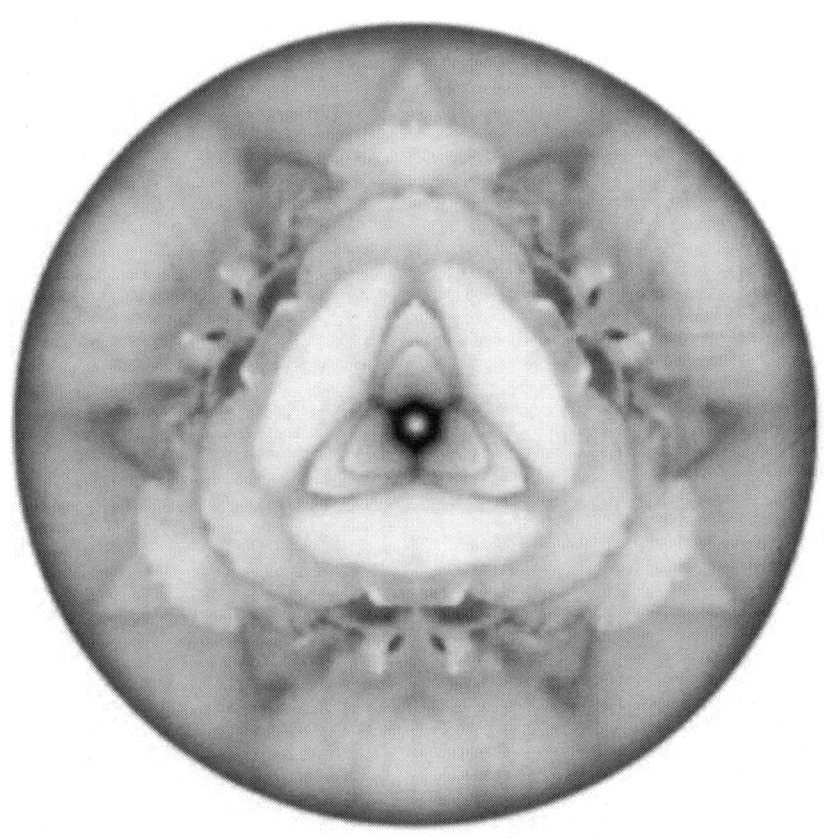

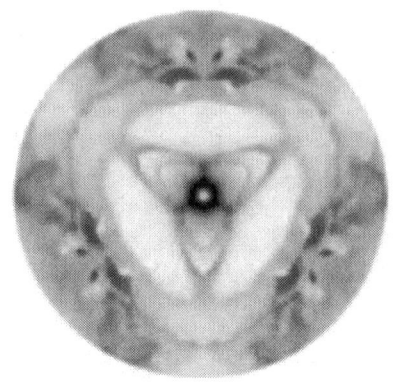

Drafted for Spiritual Work

Drafted for Spiritual Work

I called my Sisters of the Moon and asked them to come to my home soon, before our next full-moon gathering. When we met, I explained Sam's request and played the tape Jonathan had recorded. They were stunned, but not surprised that there was more to our meetings than we realized. Dory and Rose were immediately open to helping Sam make his transition to the light. Ann hesitated; she had been exposed to many new things very quickly and she initially had only attended our meetings for her own personal growth. However, we all knew she was capable of this work and, with reassurance, she agreed to participate.

I told them that Jennifer never had a chance to say good-bye to Sam and that perhaps if she did, it might help release them both. We decided I should talk to her about writing a farewell letter to Sam.

Being Jennifer's friend, I was able to kindly suggest that expressing her feelings on paper might help her heal and move on. Jennifer trusted me so she accepted that writing a good-bye letter to Sam would help her with the grief. Receiving our support would provide closure to Sam's death so she could begin to live with a more peaceful heart.

Her letter was loving and eloquent, "So this is good-bye, my darling. And as we said every night before we went to sleep, I love you more today than yesterday, but not as much as tomorrow."

With Jennifer's permission, I took her personal good-bye letter to the group. I explained that Dory, Rose, Ann, and I would pray for her and Sam's peace. Then we would burn the letter, symbolizing the release of any reluctance she felt to letting go of Sam, so he too could move forward in his new life.

The full-moon meeting to help Sam complete his transition was close in time to the date of his death two years before. My sisters and I gathered, sitting in a circle. We asked for protection and requested that only beings of the highest good be present to assist us. Dory, Rose, Ann, and I felt the divine presence of light beings around us.

We joined hands and invited Sam into the center of the circle. We *all* strongly felt his presence.

I read Jennifer's letter aloud. Her private thoughts moved us all to tears. I burned the letter in my fireplace, then sat at my piano and played the song I had written especially for Sam – *Sam's Song*. The sweet, soft, musical vibrations flowed through the room. Upon completing Sam's musical request, I rejoined the circle and felt an unexplainable gentle warmness surround me.

A magnificent light appeared above us — a luminescent, golden ray with a circular opening at the top. We all felt a *portal* opening, like an entry space between our two realms. In my mind's eye I saw Sam surrounded by the ethereal, angelic light.

Rose spoke to him saying, "Sam, go. It is time. You don't need to stay here any longer."

He was still hesitant.

Dory encouraged him. "Look up Sam. Go to the light."

Now hands were reaching out for him from the brilliant light. As we kept encouraging him, he slowly began to rise. He reached upward for the golden fingertips outstretched toward him. Reaching the top of the dazzling light, he took the hand of one of the illuminated spirits and was gone. The light became dimmer and finally faded. We wiped the tears from our cheeks. . . .

We were speechless. . . .

The Voice Across the Veil

Helping Sam transition into the light was the beginning of our *portal work* – helping souls transcend beyond Earth to the spiritual light of Creator. Some souls ascended quickly. Some needed encouragement from our side – permission to move to the light of Spirit.

At first a few souls came to one or two of my sisters and I while we were sleeping, prior to a full-moon gathering. A beautiful young woman appeared to both Rose and me in dreams. From the way she was dressed, we guessed she was from South America. This was the first time I vividly experienced someone coming to me in my dreams. She lingered very close to my face, hovering in front of me with warm and loving energy. It was not alarming in any way, it was rather soft and gentle – no words, just feelings and images in a telepathic way of communicating. She showed me an image of a woman holding her picture and, as she appeared much younger than this woman, I clearly understood it was her mother grieving over the loss of her daughter. Then I felt the young woman's sadness. She needed help and encouragement to continue her passing.

I could feel how much she wanted to ascend in the light. It seemed that as long as she lacked permission from someone – anyone – she just couldn't leave her grieving mother.

During the next gathering, she was the first to appear at the edge of our circle. As we encouraged her to enter the center of the circle, she almost ran in, so pleased, so excited. With a lovely smile she ascended without hesitation.

At every full-moon gathering during this transition work, Dory, Rose, Ann, and I all saw the same souls in our mind's eye and together were able to encourage them. We all intuitively saw, sensed, and felt the presence of those who wanted our help. I am so grateful to my sisters for their willingness to assist souls in transcending to the light.

As we continued this work during our full-moon gatherings, we discovered those who chose to remain on the Earth plane had many diverse reasons for doing so.

We also had some experiences that were not entirely peaceful. Many on the other side have multiple reasons for not leaving – they can't leave their grieving loved ones behind or some don't realize that they have crossed to the other side. Suicide victims need much help and gentle encouragement. Those that encounter an abrupt or violent end sometimes find it difficult to transition.

The next vivid experience in my dreams came in a vision of a field of yellow flowers. I saw three young girls with bright blond hair sitting together. The energy and feelings around this were frightening, and with heart pounding and panic following, my breath came in short, quick gasps.

The girl in the middle sat cross-legged, her head hanging down in shame. One of the other girls came closer to me and motioned, as if she wanted me to communicate with the young girl in the middle. As I placed my attention on her, the other two girls vanished. She appeared older now, as a teenager and I felt her extreme sadness.

"What is your name"? I communicated.

"Lucy" was the name I heard before another wave of overwhelming sadness came over me. Shame, disgrace, humiliation and unworthiness filled my heart. I knew I had to encourage Lucy to come to our circle. She was aware of our work and, although she did not feel deserving, she agreed to come.

At the full-moon circle I shared my experience with the others. As we discussed my vision, Lucy appeared. It took quite some time to get her to even enter the center of the circle. She was so bitter about her relationship with her mother and the abandonment of her boyfriend – and *so frightened* that she would not be received in good graces. I would later understand why. After two hours of gentle, loving coaxing, she finally ascended with beauty and grace.

Shortly after the experience with Lucy, during my sleep, a child appeared portraying unadulterated *horror*. She was very close to my face and all I felt was rage, resentment, violence, and terror. She looked like she was exploding. My heart pounded out of my chest; my throat closed up. I couldn't catch my breath. I was so frightened that I sent her away, but she kept reappearing — sometimes two or three times in one night and on consecutive nights.

During the time of these visions, I asked Dory to take a look at the situation with me. As we meditated, Dory said, "I see men in robes with long beards. A small child is sitting in the center of these men. She is petrified and yet there is no emotion coming from the men . . . *this little girl was forced to be a suicide bomber!*"

We didn't even wait for our meeting — we worked with her right then and there. She went quickly and my terrifying visions ceased.

After that experience, I decided not to allow nightly visitations from anyone. It wasn't necessary. Souls requesting help could appear when the portal was opened for them and not before. We would help anyone at that time and didn't need to understand their stories to do so. This type of work is based on consent and permission from all parties involved and must be honored.

As time passed, more souls came to us: a friend of Dory's, a relative of Rose's, even small groups of similar people seemed to ascend together. Then massive numbers of beings lined up to go to the light — an endless line floating upward. It was very touching to be in that highest form of energy and unconditional love at its fullest. We saw people of all races, old people, young people and children. Some people, even groups of people, like pioneers and immigrants who had died tragically, had been stuck on this plane for years. We didn't ask why they were stuck; we merely helped them move on.

The stream of souls wouldn't stop unless we stopped it. We literally had to end the process each time and explain that we would be back on the next full-moon. We always explained that no soul actually needed us to transcend: they could go at any time but we were happy to assist.

After four years of doing this work together, we all moved into new phases of our lives. Rose moved to the South with her husband. Dory began exhibiting artwork across the country and moved back to New York. Ann is concentrating on her massage therapy practice. I am creating and performing music in many forms and working with my healing practice. We don't see each other very often, but at times we still connect from our separate locations spiritually, especially to help victims of disaster.

I miss my sisters and will always keep them in my heart. There are many light workers around the world doing what we did. My sisters and I honor them.

The beautiful light is unending. The outstretched hands from the light never wavered. Religious beliefs never came up. I witnessed True unconditional love, Non-judgment in its purest form; Ultimate free-will choice. The loving All That Is, the Creator, waiting for them to return Home.

I never saw anyone turned away.

"An eerie feeling
came over me
I knew I had been
there before"

A Dream Relived

A Dream Relived

I remember lives from centuries ago: in ancient Asia, as a royal Egyptian during the time of Christ, as a young girl of the Aztec people, a woman during the sixteenth century Renaissance, an Amish teacher, a Medieval male page; and in Tahiti, Africa and Salem, Massachusetts, where Dory was my sister during the infamous witch hunts.

I continued working with Jonathan Westley, and each time we spoke I gained more enlightenment. Spirits of light and a multitude of good souls, whom I felt were my spirit guides, discussed my past lives. The sessions were illuminating and practical. I began to understand more clearly the connections between my past lives and my current life circumstances and choices.

After one particular session, I began having dreams of a past life as a Native American. Then the visions of this past life during meditation became more like scenes from a movie. I saw myself as a woman of the tribe, standing on a hill and looking down in great anguish at a bloody massacre of my people, sighing heavily. With my blanket wrapped around me, I spread my arms out in enormous grief then pulled the blanket tightly to me. I had known this would happen; why did they not listen to me? I turned and walked away in immense sorrow.

Soon after these dreams and visions, friends of my family invited us to visit a Native American encampment site west of our home in Colorado. Heather, my daughter, was thirteen years old at the time. With the help of our friends, we found tepee rings, arrowheads, and chipped or carved handmade tools such as scrapers made from obsidian, quartz, flint and churt.

An eerie feeling came over me. I knew I had been there before, and after this one-day trip I wanted to go back.

Fortunately my family was eager to return as well and we made several follow-up visits. I found empty water reservoirs with rocks piled around to hold pools of water on a downhill slope. A river, now only a trickle of water, had once flowed through the valley. On one side of the river, flat rocks in semi-circular patterns covered the mountainside. On a slope across the stream from the tepee rings rested a large mound covered with weathered, black cinders mixed with earth.

To the left, a cluster of pine trees sheltered an area. In

my mind's eye I saw Indian women and children working and playing, tanning hides and making useful things for everyday life. The children were learning crafts from the women. As I approached the area, I noticed a small, flat piece of yellow quartz lying on top of a cluster of stiff, pale-green buffalo grass – as if someone wanted me to find it. With two serrated sides and a notch on one end, it looked like a tiny scraper used for cutting and detailing. When I picked it up, a chill rushed through me and a memory flashed. *This once belonged to me.*

"Thank you, Spirit."

Naming the spot "Sacred Ground," I made an offering to the earth in exchange for taking the tool off the land. With great reverence I gave thanks to Mother Earth for the gift.

The next Christmas, at a holiday gathering, I shared my memory of this magical place with a family friend. He excitedly told me of a segment in a documentary he saw on television about interesting places to explore in Colorado. They mentioned the same area, describing the location, directions and name of the creek that flowed through the valley. Not only Native American artifacts were discovered but even Civil War buttons had been found there. I attempted to locate the television station to get a copy of the documentary but was unable to do so.

I visited the Colorado History museum, contacted the

Colorado Historical Society and the Division of Wildlife to research more information. All confirmed many official archeological findings in the area.

The Past Reawakened

The Past Reawakened

The following October, I attended a retreat in Sedona, Arizona, with Jonathan Westly, not knowing that it would take me even closer to understanding the Indian life that so strongly pursued me.

Jonathan was hosting the weekend retreat and asked if I would provide background piano music for his wife Kara's meditations. An entire night of music under the stars was scheduled, as many musicians were in attendance. Jonathan asked if I would accompany the vocalists and also perform my own compositions. He encouraged me to bring copies of my new CD to sell while performing.

We began on Friday evening and planned to stay through Monday, enjoying this warm autumn weekend in northern Arizona. A generous couple in Oak Creek Canyon offered the grounds of their lovely home for the retreat – an old bed and breakfast inn nestled beside a river. Our group of twenty-seven women and three men met outside in the spacious yard, surrounded by lush green pine trees, hiking trails, regal mountains and red rocks towering into the blue sky. It was an ideal setting for the retreat's theme – connecting with nature.

We entered the verdant, green yard before dark and sat down under a misting canopy facing an arch of vines with tiny white Christmas lights woven throughout.

We were asked to introduce ourselves and explain why we were attending the retreat. The participants came from all over the United States, California to New York. A man from Phoenix named Evan, of average height with short brown hair and blue eyes, humorously said, "I'm here because my wife wanted me to come."

By the time we finished introductions, it was fully dark. The balmy Arizona night air was warm and pleasant. The stars twinkled in the sky. The only other light came from the tiny, white lights on the vines.

Kara led a powerful meditation, guiding the participants into an inner vision of their own sensory experiences and tapping into their own beings.

I accompanied Kara on a digital piano Jonathan had set up in the yard, improvising with soft, soothing, peaceful background music that flowed through me.

As I played, I scanned the serene faces of the group. Everyone had closed their eyes, except Evan, who, I noticed, was staring at me. I continued playing the piano, but, still feeling Evan staring, I turned to him and smiled. No response. He seemed blank. Curious, I nodded and smiled again. He seemed startled, but smiled back.

After the meditation, we broke for the evening and went to our various accommodations along the canyon.

Saturday offered glorious weather as we arrived back at the outdoor site of our meeting place. My music, *Celebration of Light*, played on a portable stereo. After a short meditation, we divided into four Jeeps for an arranged tour of the famous vortexes in the region — collectively one of the eleven spiritual "power points" on the planet.

We drove along winding mountain roads through pine and pinon trees. Sunshine caressed the great red rock sculptures that soared against the bright blue sky. Our tour guides were very knowledgeable about the Native American history that enriches the area, as Sedona is regarded a sacred place by Native Americans.

We visited several of the major vortexes, one of which had many medicine wheels scattered throughout the area. In Native American spirituality, the Medicine Wheel represents harmony and connections and is considered a major symbol of peaceful interaction among all living beings on Earth. I felt a chill again remembering the life that haunted me.

After a presentation conducted by our tour guides, we

had some time to explore privately. I walked down a path and found myself surrounded by medicine wheels of all sizes. Stepping into one of the circles I drifted into a short but meaningful meditation – connecting with the earth, sky, wind, and spirit of the area. I sat immersed in my own personal thoughts when suddenly I saw faces – faces of Native American people, *my people*, surrounding me. What did this mean?

I meandered along a trail back toward the Jeeps, drawn by soothing flute music played by one of the tour guides. We returned to our meeting place in Oak Creek Canyon for the rest of the day's activities, and then broke for dinner.

After dinner we gathered at the main house for the evening of entertainment under the stars and the twinkling lights. Three of us performed on piano. I accompanied several vocalists and others sang and accompanied themselves on guitar. The music flowed serenely, winding through the warm summer night air. This was actually the first time in several years that I had performed in public. Jonathan made it clear I only needed to participate to my comfort level. I realized that if I could improvise and not perform a structured piece, I was able to do it and actually enjoy it!

Sunday we spent time along the river. When we returned I ran into Evan.

He was holding my CD.

"I love your music," he said.

"Thank you."

"I know you," he said, hesitantly.

"No, I don't think we've met before."

"Did you ever work in the Phoenix area?"

"No. Never."

"I know you from somewhere."

Evan was so insistent, so sure, that I suggested we meditate on it together sometime in the afternoon.

Quietly he said, "Yes, I'd like that."

At days end I looked for Evan. I found him walking along the riverbank with his wife, Fiona. I felt uneasy going up to a perfect stranger and dragging him off to meditate, but my curiosity was strong; I felt there was something I needed to know.

On the patio behind the house, Evan and I sat facing each other and then took hands. We decided to use guided imagery to help us visualize when we might have met. I was curious to see if it was in a past life.

"Picture this. A beautiful valley surrounded by mountains."

Immediately, Evan described the details I recognized. "I'm back to a time in the west." he said. "I see mountains. There's an open space surrounded by tall pine and aspen trees and a small creek running through the middle of what appears to be a large encampment. On one side of the camp, I see a large group of tepees. One is larger than the rest. Now I'm inside the tepee. There's an angry discussion going on. Some sort of Council meeting, several men and one woman, maybe she's a medicine woman. She is sitting on the ground with the men, wearing a deer-hide dress with a beaded pattern across the top in a half moon shape. Across from her, a young warrior sits, also dressed in hides. He is waving his hands, trying to make a point and looking very angry. She attempts to speak, but he silences her. She is walking outside . . . the woman is you, Sue."

I saw everything Evan described and turned cold with realization. It was my dream, my visions, my Sacred Ground.

Evan continued, "Now you are speaking to a large gathering of people and chanting. You are warning of doom and devastation if they fight, saying peace is the only answer." The vision continued with a long period of chanting to the people as a premonition of what was to come.

After a long silence, Evan and I finally dropped hands and stood. "What an incredible experience!" he said. "We shared the same life. I was watching from inside the teepee."

I nodded. *Tangible evidence.*

"Evan, the place in the vision, I know where it is."

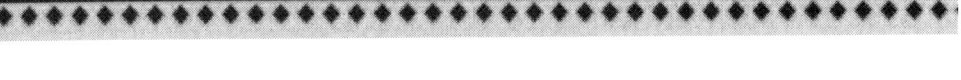

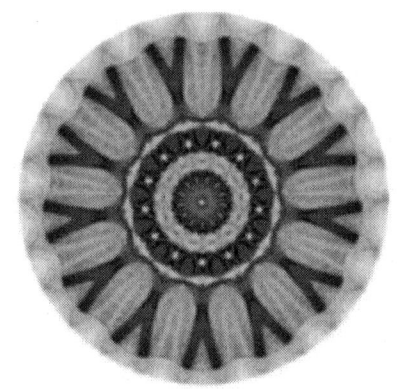

Released from the Past

Released from the Past

My past as a Native American woman surfaced throughout my life. As a child living in the Midwest, I drew pictures of mountains, even though I had never seen one. I was fixated on horses, even though I had never been near one. Whenever I saw or heard anything about Native Americans, I *knew* what their lives were like. As I grew older, I had flashes of myself with darker skin and long dark hair. I knew I had lived a life as a Native American woman.

As the information about my Native American lifetime unfolded, it became more and more intriguing. I received visions in meditations and information each time I visited the land. At times, I felt overcome with sadness, realizing that something dreadful happened there. It felt as though I had transcended time.

In the encampment at Sacred Ground, everyone loved and appreciated each other. Respecting each person was a common practice of the tribe. Everyone had responsibilities and completed their tasks with joy. I had a sister and I loved her very much. She had a devoted husband and two sons.

I appeared to be learning to become a medicine woman and spent a lot of time gathering herbs; the land was abundant with many varieties of plants and roots. I also assisted the shaman of the tribe in various ceremonies. My name was Running Bear.

The shaman of the tribe was a strong and powerful man. I sensed a connection with him, possibly as a teacher, friend, or both. I realized Evan in this life was the shaman.

Running Bear was promised in marriage to a young warrior. I felt very distressed by this—even in the vision—and knew I didn't want to be his wife. It appeared that his intentions were self-serving as the impression was that I was the daughter of a chief. Knowing my displeasure, the young warrior felt great animosity toward me.

One sunny day, in a meadow of wildflowers and tall grasses, I saw my sister and I laughing blissfully, holding hands and dancing in a circle. Meanwhile in the woods, some of the other women and children were happily gathering food when they were brutally attacked by soldiers. We rushed toward them after hearing their screams but arrived too late. Many were critically wounded. The tribesmen transported the injured back to camp on travois pulled by horses. The two of us worked feverishly alongside the shaman, trying to patch wounds and save as many as we could.

After that horrendous event, I saw myself sitting with the shaman, my friend, discussing what could be done. I knew the soldiers would come back and felt strongly that peace was the only answer—fearing that if we fought back more would die. I pleaded with him to encourage the elders not to fight.

For some reason, I was involved with the tribal Council, perhaps as a seer. The young warrior that proposed marriage to me, and who I saw in the first vision with Evan, was also in attendance—opposing everything I stood for. I could sense extreme conflict in the energy between us. The warrior wanted retaliation. The shaman convinced the tribal council to meet with the white leaders to discuss terms for peace. That infuriated the warrior even more. He blamed me for persuading the shaman to act on the side of peace and he felt humiliated.

A few weeks later, in the large Council Lodge, the elders met with the white leaders. A fire burned in the center as they sat in a circle, engaging in a pipe ceremony in hopes that such a tragedy would never happen again.

The young warrior never forgave me for his humiliation. His rage and hatred festered. One afternoon, as I walked along a trail among the aspen trees, I came upon the warrior. In my youthful lack of insight, I confronted him. The warrior became incensed. Violence was his retribution. I witnessed myself as Running Bear lying on the ground bloodied and severely brutalized.

I was sitting in the cold water of the river, tending my wounds, when the shaman came upon me. I was badly injured and could barely move. It appeared to take a long time to heal, but he and my sister were able to nurse me back to health.

When news of the warrior's attack on me became public, the Council shunned him for a period of time. No one was to talk to him, or even look at him. The disgrace only further enraged him as he blamed me for causing his pain and embarrassment. As time passed, however, his rage inflamed revenge toward the white soldiers and he goaded the other young warriors on to battle. Opposing my stance for peace was his vindication.

Over time I found myself again inside the Council Lodge. I saw a beaded medicine bag and objects placed on the ground in front of me in specific positions of importance. Once again, my enemy, the young warrior sat across from me, seething with anger, as he proposed war on the soldiers to defend the honor of the people.

The Council leaders tried to convince him that we were outnumbered, but the young warrior would not back down.

He stormed outside and shouted his case to the people who had gathered to hear the Council's decision. The warrior argued in favor of fighting, trying to convince the people to follow him. He promised them safety, as he had warriors to protect them. I pleaded the case for peace to the people that had gathered; when they would not listen, I chanted a telling story that forewarned of doom if they were not careful in their decision. (The first vision Evan and I had in Sedona).

Nevertheless, about thirty people chose to follow the impetuous young warrior, approximately one-fourth of the community. They packed and left – my sister, her husband and two sons along with them. I was devastated at the thought of what might happen. Even during this vision I felt physically shaken.

On that fateful day, not far from the original encampment, the warrior led his followers into an ambush. I was the first to reach the gruesome site. Blood, blood everywhere. All dead. I stared, looking down at my loved ones from the top of the hill. With painful, searing tears streaming down my face I pulled my blanket tightly around me and cried, "Why wouldn't they listen to me?" I turned away, grief-stricken.

Those of us left mourned for our dead and held a

traditional burial ceremony – a funeral pyre built up on a stack of logs – at the very place I could not bring myself to step upon in this lifetime – the cinder mound.

Two had survived the ambush: my sister, critically wounded and left for dead, and the warrior leader. As the large fire rose into the sky, he rode away into the distance with his head hanging in shame and disgrace.

Soon afterward the soldiers once again banded together on the outskirts of the encampment. Shocked, I watched the army of soldiers ride through the camp, wielding their guns, shooting anyone in sight. The women and children were running; and in the midst of their screams and terror, I witnessed myself being shot in the back and falling to the ground . . . dying . . . dead.

Was this past life memory given to me in such detail for a reason? Was I guided to the very spot it happened to fulfill some sort of purpose? Did I make a promise to come back in this way to heal something or someone?

During my many visits to Sacred Ground, I always felt the presence of my people. I stood there one cloudless, sunny day and reverently prayed to Great Spirit in gratitude and thanksgiving for guiding my path and helping those who could not leave understand there is assistance on this side.

On the same beautiful, hot, sunny day, as I finished my prayer, a huge clap of thunder rolled across the top of the mountains and shook the ground beneath my feet. At that moment I knew the souls who were trapped there had ascended to the light. The area felt lighter, as if remembering, compassion, and gratitude had assisted in clearing the trauma which had obscured the brightness of this valley for far too long.

The memories no longer haunt me. I did what needed to be done. However, my connection with that lifetime will always be a part of me. Running Bear remains inside of me.

Souls lost for a time – treacheries hidden for a time can be restored by remembering what once was. Remembering is a gift because it gives us an opportunity to heal and to forgive the past not only for ourselves, but for our past generations – even past lifetimes – so that we may furthermore learn not to harm again, or hold onto grief, or carry dark anger. Such grievous sadness and distress are a plague to our consciousness, destroying what can be ours: Life in harmony with an unburdened mind and an accepting free heart.

Part II

"Inside each one of you
is a beautiful being,
created in perfection,
waiting to be
discovered."

Sacred Friends

Sacred Friends

Sacred friends come in all forms, young and old. I have walked with an elderly gentleman through his crossing and have been visited by young ones I knew in this life who departed too quickly, learning from each one of them. One of my dearest and most exceptional sacred friends is a sixteen-year-old girl named Emma.

My daughter, Heather, was a sophomore in high school when she met Emma. She was coaching a volleyball camp for the middle school and Emma was on her team. Even though Emma was two years younger than Heather, they connected right away. By the time Emma entered high school, the two girls embarked on a sisterly friendship.

As I spent time with Emma, I observed wisdom about this young person that went deeper than her chronological age. She was the most loving, kind, forgiving soul and touched the heart of everyone she met. She had a way of making everyone feel they had a special part in her life.

We spent a lot of time together at track meets and volleyball games. She sometimes enjoyed being with us parents more than the other kids. She was physically beautiful, but her inner beauty radiated a unique kindness that was unexplainable. Her smile would melt your heart. A typical teenager, she loved her family and friends, music and cars. She participated in athletics, on the speech team, and she was a good student. But there was more about this unique human being – to know her was to love her – that is all I can say.

The last time I spent with Emma was a Friday night at the 2006 high school homecoming volleyball game. Heather came home from college for the weekend and we all went to support the team. Emma chose not to play volleyball that year, but she was there. It was fun to see her again and just spend a little time together.

I will never forget the following Wednesday – a day that would change the lives of an entire community and touch an entire country.

Heather called me from her student union center around noon. I heard her panicked voice say, "Turn on the TV! Someone has taken hostages at the high school and he has a gun! Mom, I'm so worried – I know Emma is in that class!"

I immediately turned on the television. In disbelief I watched the events unfold. Seven hostages were taken with no rhyme or reason for it. Some twisted individual released one girl at a time. No one knew who exactly was in that room. Two girls were left – gunshots rang out – one was carried out on a stretcher and taken away in the Flight for Life helicopter. I knew it was Emma.

I also knew she was gone instantaneously. My heart sank. The gunman was shot, or shot himself, immediately after shooting Emma in the head. Two people were dead. One was completely innocent. We were stunned, speechless. Why? Why did he choose to do something so dreadful, so horrible – so devastating?

And why Emma?

I was numb. The reality of it was too awful to grasp. My heart ached for Emma's family, friends, and community. The effect rippled throughout our small town and out into the world. People came together in their grief and sadness, trying to ease the gnawing pain that tore deep into their souls. People across the country were empathizing, wanting to help in some way and not quite knowing how.

The grief was overwhelming, yet the people in Emma's life were again the example she lived. Instead of reacting out of fear and anger, her parents, twin brother and family friends turned this horrific event into a message of kindness – which completely embodied Emma. The last communication with her parents via text message was "I love you guys". These incredible people took that message and gave Emma a farewell befitting to her in the most eloquent and powerful way. Music is a big part of this group of people and they played their instruments and sang from their hearts and souls in honor of their loved one. On behalf of Emma they embraced the world with kindness, requesting that we all perform random acts of kindness for Emma.

News coverage of the event swept the entire country. President Bush spoke of the devastating incident and of the request for random acts of kindness brought forth by Emma's family and closest friends on national television. Gentleness overcame our small community unlike anything I had experienced before.

This is Emma's initial message to teach the world kindness through her family and friends.

So how do we release the pain – the empty hole in the heart? Especially when it involves senseless, insane violence. How do we continue on with life?

We connect with others in love. We share their sorrow. We lighten their load a little and therefore lighten our own. The lesson is so simple and yet so powerful – we become kinder to one another. How thoughtful, how profound. *Be kind. Love one another.* When we do that, a type of peace emerges. We begin to heal our own hearts because we are touching other hearts. We become more concerned for others than for ourselves – in a good way – and this brings about peace. We begin to reflect the innate goodness in ourselves and in each other.

This inner peace begins changing the world, not on a massive scale, but by touching one by one, focusing our strengths, goodness and kindness and by seeing and honoring these attributes in each soul who walks the earth. One by one, we create random acts of kindness. As we consciously behave in this way we will release the need for judgment, jealousy, pettiness and all other human qualities that block the way to giving and receiving love.

We all have these capabilities. We all can be our authentic selves. We can raise our children in this manner. As we increase our awareness, we will see great change in the way we view and treat all living things – the earth, the plants and the animals. We *can* walk on this planet in honor of it all. We are capable of honoring all individuals for who and what they really are – creations in the light of Spirit.

"We must learn to love,
we must learn to be kind"

All

Embracing

Love

All Embracing Love

When Emma first came to me in my dreams, I was thrilled to see her, to communicate again in this way. She has much to say and is working hard to get her messages across. All of the messages received have been transcribed from automatic writing or tape recordings. As I later worked on transcribing the tape recordings I realized that Emma's personality came through her voice (or my voice should I say as I was channeling her). Light, bouncy and a bit mischievous.

The following is the first message to come through using automatic writing:

"Do not be afraid of this type of communication as this also has been planned for some time. Sue, the one I speak through now, agreed to this a long time ago when she stood before the seven spirits saying "Yes, I can and will do it if I have your help!" She did not bring this about. WE collectively did during another time and place. (This is recognized as a soul agreement.) It is all a part of the grand scheme of things. And it is also beautiful. My meeting Heather, my mom working with Sue on her CD cover, *Sacred Friends*, even Heather creating the event in the hospital because she was pushing on Sue's appendix during birth. There are no mistakes. There are no coincidences. There is a reason for everything that happens in life."

Four days after Emma's memorial service she came to visit me in my dreams. I remember being exhausted that evening so I merely acknowledged her and tried to go back to sleep. That particular evening Emma would not leave me alone. She kept showing up and insisting to speak with me. I got up and moved to the living room, curious what could be so urgent.

As I sat in meditation, I noticed Emma seemed very concerned. She wanted me to help remove the dark energy of the man who caused the tragedy. She was referring to the school and the entire community and stated that none of us would be able to begin healing if this darkness remained. It needed to be cleared out.

My immediate thought was of Dory, not only because of our work together, but also because of her connection with Emma. Emma worked for Dory as an assistant in her art studio. I felt that we needed at least one more person to help and when I spoke to Dory about the situation, she suggested Trish. Trish and her husband are the ones Emma refers to as her "aunt and uncle".

Within a couple of days the three of us met at my home. As we gathered outside under a tall, sturdy Ponderosa pine tree, Dory shared some of her insights with us. She said we needed to gain a wider vision – that perceived reality is in the eyes of the beholder and therefore truth. We needed to change the only constant and not let primal fears and arrogant assumptions interject into the overall picture. I must admit I was a little confused by these statements. I don't think any of us had a clear picture of what was about to happen. My only thought was to get rid of the dark energy, as far away as we could, but I also trusted Dory and her intuitive wisdom.

We started by surrounding our circle with the protection of the white light and asked that we be assisted only by those of the highest goodness. As we began our personal connections with one another, Emma appeared, happy and eager to be there, to watch what was about to happen. We did not allow her to enter the circle but were pleased to have her hold sacred space as the fourth one of the group. Ironically, the empty space was to the west, in Native American medicine circles, the place of strength, experience and introspection (spirit beings).

We called on the man responsible for the tragic heartache of the community. He slithered in to the circle with a seemingly dark presence, his face pointed down toward the earth. I began, "You must leave this area. You cannot stay here." The energy was foreboding, sinister.

"Why?" said Trish. "Why would you do this?"

He spoke through me; "They knew what I would never have." Although he was speaking through me, Dory was picking up on his feelings. She began shaking, crying. "He was terribly abused, ill-treated and extremely disturbed as a result," she said. "He had failed relationships and learned from an early age that he could not trust anyone."

"Why this, why now?" we asked.

"All these girls were so beautiful and they would grow to have wonderful lives. They would be happy and have families of their own. They would love and be loved. I would never have experienced anything like that in this life. They knew love." He pointed at Emma. "She knew it the most, the best. She was love. I was so jealous, so envious. She knew love from the time of her birth and she would share that love throughout her life with others – all others except someone like me," he said.

The three of us sat there weeping. Even *he* saw the love that Emma exuded. Dory began, "You must change your perception, your reality, if you are to leave us in peace – and you *must* leave. Go back to the time of your birth. See yourself in your mother's arms. She is holding you and rocking you. Feel her love surround you."

"I can't," he responded.

"You must. We are only looking at your perceived reality and that is being in your mother's arms as a baby." When we set the intention of allowing our reality to be changed, it becomes so – therefore the perception becomes reality.

Trish said, "There is something he wants to say. There is something he wants to hear. Sue, what does he want to hear?"

At that point all I could see was the dark soul – his face pointing toward the ground.

"Pain, pain – I'm in so much pain," he spoke quietly.

After a long pause, Trish said "I know what it is. He wants to hear 'I love you.' Maybe he had never heard those words in his tormented life. I love you."

I looked at those amazing women with reverence and honor. They experienced excruciating pain at the great loss of Emma's beautiful spirit, yet they continued to surround the perverse soul with the unconditional love of Creator.

Above us a portal began to open. "Look up," I said. "Go toward the light."

His face turned up slightly as he said, "How can you do this, I don't deserve it. How and why would you do this?"

It wasn't about our personal feelings – of course we had no feelings of love for this murderer. It was profoundly about the love of Divine Source – because hatred melts in the face of love.

"You can't stay here, you must go!" I said. We continued to pour unconditional love – the love of All That Is into the dark soul before us. It embarrassed, humiliated, touched, and confused him. Then, in all his pain and anguish, embarrassment and humiliation, he looked up and reached for the outstretched hands beckoning to him. He floated up through the portal and the darkness was released from our earthly plane.

The dark soul that was released saw Emma's light. He wanted to crush it and yet he wanted to know what it was like to love and be loved unconditionally. He was amazed and frightened by the women who were honoring Emma's request. "Why? Why would they do such a thing when I did not deserve even the notion of it?" he thought.

The strength and actions of these women took away the power – his power. It diminished him and did the opposite of his intention to terrorize, cause fear and hatred. He ascended because there was nothing of his darkness left but a shell.

Wanting to protect her loved ones, Emma knew this would be the result. She also knew most would not understand or accept dealing with her perpetrator in this way. And the three of us possessed the understanding to do what needed to be done.

We didn't have to feel we were betraying or being disloyal to Emma or those who loved her, because we knew he had to leave the earth plane and we acted accordingly. We were merely honoring Emma's request. As we heaped unconditional love upon the perverse soul, it negated all he strived for.

As we left the shelter of the wise, old Ponderosa pine tree, I heard Emma whisper, "I would like you to help me ascend in the light soon."

Later, in meditation, I asked Emma to explain her concept of the event she orchestrated to remove the dark soul from the Earth plane.

"Would you like to share with us Emma?" I asked

"Oh yes. I sat on the side line and was *so* proud of Sue, Dory and Trish – so proud it cannot be put into words. It is not about forgiveness as much as the fact that I wanted to remove the darkness from the area of the community."

"Where is he now?" I asked.

"He is in a place far away from this realm. It would not be good to have him this close to the earth plane either. They are working with him. All are welcome to ascend, but all are not automatically received into the light plane. All are received in love but if they are dark, tormented, disturbed, they go to a place where they can't bother us in this realm. It was good for him to go – his darkness would have wreaked havoc on earth as well. I *don't like* him," Emma said very strongly, "although I have love for every creation. There is a difference."

Two weeks later, I knew it was time. I called Dory and Trish. We invited Joni upon Emma's request. She is the mom of one of her friends and quite knowledgeable in the ways of our ceremonies.

As we sat in our circle and began preparing to assist Emma, our tears began to flow. It was difficult to let her go. We all shared the comfort of having her around. "Are you here Emma?" I asked.

"Yes," replied Emma speaking through me. "Do not be sad. It is a beautiful thing that you do – helping souls go to the light. Many wish to stay with their loved ones but their light grows dim, they need to move forward. Please help me go, help me stand in my light.

"I did not go through this to have my message changed. It is about hands reaching out to one another in kindness. My message is of love. It is very strong. It must be heard. It must not be mungled up!

"I love all of my family and friends. I wish I could mention all of them – no one should be less. I want to come back and it is my *mission* to come back and be with all of you.

"Trish, you understand my message of love. It is why this has all been played out in this way. It was my choice to live, love, and leave in this way. It is why all of our lives have been intertwined. Not through grief and sadness, but through all that is good.

"It is the power of the feminine that must be strong. It is okay for them (the men) to do the business. Please try to help keep it focused; even though they like to protect me. Even now they would like to put me in a little bubble. They must know that it is from *me*. They must know that this was my choice. Keep the message clear. It is LOVE. I love you all . . ."

"We love you Emma," we repeated through our tears. The brightest portal Dory and I had ever seen opened. Many hands reached down for this very special being. With a huge smile, and in her pink and gold light, she rose up into the brilliance – Emma style – with love, joy, and delight.

Ethereal Messages

Ethereal Messages

A few months after Emma transcended, I was introduced to a psychotherapist named Kris who worked with a technique that was very successful for Post Traumatic Stress Disorder – called EMDR. We quickly became friends and she offered her technique to keep me focused and expand my ability to communicate by channeling for longer periods of time. I had no idea I was dancing on the edge of discovering new remarkable techniques that physically heal and clear limitations and trauma that keep us from living in our brightest potential.

We recorded each session. Emma's presence was very apparent and her light beautiful voice came through with the confidence and clarity of her bright spirit.

"Are you happy, Emma?"

"Yes, I am so happy! It is so beautiful here."
"Where are you?"
"I'm in heaven."
"Who are you with?"
"Many. My Grandpa. He helps me, he is with me. He has walked through this time with me. And Sam. We met upon my passing."
"What side of your family is your Grandpa from?"
"My mom's. He was her grandpa too."
"What is the temperature like there?"
"Very comfortable – not too hot, or cold."
"What day is it?"
"There are no days. We do not go by time as you do there."
"Are there structures, buildings, houses?"
"It's more like beautiful gardens and open expansive clouds and beauty – beauty everywhere you look."
"What do people do there?"
"I spend much time trying to be with my family, to help them to not feel so sad."
"Do you speak with them?"
"I try very hard"
"Do they hear you?"
"No. But I also visit my friends. Some of them like to play with me in their dreams."
"That is probably when you can connect with them the best, when they are dreaming. Then you seem real to them."

"Yes and some others can acknowledge me!"
"Do you sleep?"
"No."
"Do you know what happened to you?"
"Yes. Death – he shot me in the head."
"Why?"
"I don't know. I know I tried to break away from him and he got mad."
"Did you know he would do that?"
"Yeah, I knew. I thought we were both going to be killed."
"The other hostage?"
"Yeah, but he was shot. I'm not sure how it happened, but she got away."
"Did it hurt?"
"No. It was instantaneous."
"What would you like to say to your family?"
"I love you guys so much, again, please keep my message clear, Emma continued. "The message is love, the message is kindness, the message is to share with others and touch each others' hearts. It is not about what they do, it is about what they feel."
"What happened when you were shot? Did someone come to get you?"
"Oh, yes. Many were there immediately to help guide me through it. I had fun, though, during this intermittent time. I visited with many on your side.

Many could talk to me and we did talk and had fun. We laughed and cried together."

"What would you like to say to your friends?"

"I love all of them. I wish they wouldn't be sad."

"What message of hope can you give to them so they won't be sad?"

"I am not dead. I want them to know *I am not dead.* I want them to stop thinking of me as just being dead. I am *alive.* I am here and I can be here for them and with them."

"Do you know anything about the future?"

"It is my message. We must learn to love. We must learn to be kind. We must learn to live in that way."

"That's a great message. How do we do that? Do you know?"

"By each person living and being in that kindness and honoring each other. Honoring each other with the respect they deserve no matter where they are in life. No matter what walk of life they have."

"Do you see any famous people?"

"I see many, but it is not as awesome as it is over there."

"Who most of all would you like to have hear this message from you?"

"My family. My family encompasses a broad range of people. Relatives, of course, but my friendships of all ages are my extended families as well."

"Have you seen anyone die recently?"

"Oh, yes."

"Do you know them?"

"I helped, I help *them*."

"Who do you help?"

"I help, as we say, the "four healing mothers." It was Dory's relative. She died of cancer. She was sixteen. She just couldn't fight anymore. I just came and put my arm around her and we went off."

"Did you help her adjust?"

"Yeah."

"Who are the 'four healing mothers?' "

"Sue and Dory, they have worked together for a long time. Auntie Trish and Joni too, they were like moms to me. I love them."

"What do you get to do next?"

"I don't know. I'm still trying to help my family."

"Maybe this message will help them. Do you have a teacher?"

"Yes, there are many. They show me things and teach me things.

"Who?"

"The Light Beings, Angels, Guides and Grandpa."

"Will you come back in another body?"

"Eventually."

"What will you do in the meantime?"

"Help others. I help when they cross. I help them as they come into this area."

"What do you do to help them?"

"I let them know not to be afraid."

"Have you made a lot of friends there?"

"Oh yes! Everyone is loving. Everyone is kind and unconditional. There is no judgment. There is no jealousy. Everyone is happy for being together."

"What do you do to make them feel happy to be there when they arrive?"

"It isn't like words, it's more like feelings. We don't really speak in words in this way. It is more like telepathy, as you would say, but it isn't just mental – it is also physical. It's a feeling . . . like a big ball of love."

"Have you heard of the term synergistic energy exchange, Emma?"

"That's what it is!"

"Can you speak of the agreement, the contract that we made?" I asked.

"As each of us plan our lives out at the time of creation we make contracts, agreements that will be played out in the physical form. That's not to say that you cannot change these circumstances through choice. Free will choice is always present. We were all brought together for this purpose."

"Who?"

"All of the ones we have interacted with in this lifetime. All that are a part of this story. Again, I am not dead. There is life after physical death and it is beautiful."

"What can you share with us about the other side?"

"We are all here. There are different realms, as on earth different religious philosophies. But there is only one Source – we are all part of it – though we fit in our own certain places. It is becoming easier now to communicate as the veil is becoming thinner. Many still have fear and disbelief. That is one reason I agreed to depart in this way to receive national attention – to begin by showing the world that even through painful, unreasonable, horrific acts, mankind can shine. I am so proud of my family and friends. They too agreed to this situation to teach the world that kindness and love are the keys to life on this planet."

"Do you have more messages to share Emma?"

"Yes. LOVE, LOVE, LOVE – it can't be said enough. Think hard about your choices, as they make huge differences in the long run. As we become more connected with each other in a spiritual way, our loving thoughts alone will begin to make a shift in the consciousness of the world. We can heal the earth just by our loving thoughts and intentions. As we change our perceptions, we will consciously change the way we live. We will come back into balance and harmony with the earthly plane. It seems almost impossible now, but it CAN be done!"

Emma continued:

"We are more evolved than ever at this point. Mom, you can talk to me any time. I am always there – holding your feet. Can't you feel me? I know you do, but then you dismiss it as unreal. I am with all of you at times, holding you in loving support. You have so much support from this side.

"It is realized that it is easy to make agreements in a place where there is only bliss. We grow from each experience, by each choice we make during these lifetimes – whether they are what you would judge good or bad. It is merely a choice and that choice creates the next set of circumstances.

"Yes, I agreed to this "death" contract and afterward felt some sadness because I missed my family and friends – even my physical body – but I am so excited to tell you that I am right here, right now! *I am not dead!*

"There is not one thing out of balance here. The male-female energy is perfection. There is no struggle for dominance. All is perfection. All is beauty. All is as it could be on Earth."

"My twin, my mirror image in male form, is a small example of that which is balance on both sides. Please do not step away from your feelings, my brother – express them, feel them all. It is only the perceived reality that is made into truth. Perceive yourself whole, unshattered, and willing to open to life and love. It can be done. I am here for you always.

"Daddy, you are so logical; I know that's how you deal, cope. I'm so glad it was you that received my last message on earth. I love you – I love you all.

"Those of you that I felt so close to, as if you were blood relatives, I honor and salute you. I love you for being who you are, for capturing the essence of my message. I refer to you now as my aunt and uncle to help you understand how much I love you.

"I must go for now. Thank you for helping me get my message across. We will talk again soon."

"Thank you, Emma. Is Sam there with you now?"

"Oh, yeah, he is right here."

"Yes, I am here. It is nice to have voice again." This time Sam's voice appeared to have a wise and new found assurance in it since our last communication.

"What have you learned?"

"It is so beautiful here, so gorgeous and incredibly wonderful. I have waited all my life to see God. God is incredibly gorgeous."

"What does God look like?"

"Gorgeous."

"What does God feel like?"

"Like nothing you could ever experience on your side."

"So you have seen God?"

"We all do."

"Is there Goddess?"

"One is the same as the other."

"Just depends on your point of view, Sam?"

"Yes."

"Is there anything that you would like to say to your wife?"

"That I do love her. I will always love her and I will wait for her as long as it takes. We will be together again. She is a very beautiful being and I am very proud of her and my daughters. They grow more beautiful each day. I have so much love for them. She does not understand these things completely as she is very caught up in her own beliefs. This is not bad because it gives them hope – if it gives them hope and comfort, does it really hurt?"

"Are you talking about religion?"

"Yes, very much so."

"What have you learned from God?"

"God is creator of all things. God is unconditional. God forgives and does not judge. Each experience that each individual has on the planet is expressly for the experience, for the growth of each soul.

"Is there good and bad?"

"There just is."

"How far away is heaven?"

"A snap of a finger, a blink of an eye."

"Is there hell?'

"Again, it is choice. If one chooses to be of the dark, it is not judged; it is choice."

"Is it a matter of belief that you go where you think you are going to go, Sam?"

"No, not at all."

"So why would someone choose to go to hell?"

"If all is created in God, what is not of God's creation?"

"If God does not judge, why would there be a hell?"

"I did not say there was a hell."

"Are there ghosts on this earth?"

"Yes, very much so. Many."

"Why."

"They are merely souls that cannot leave their families, just as I was at one time. Some are stuck for many reasons. It is why I initially called on the help of those on your side to facilitate my progress and to ask for assistance to help others."

"Do you have teachers?"

"Oh, yes. There is much to learn here. We have all understanding. We have the memory from the time of creation and we see not only where we have been this time around, but where we have been many other times as well."

"When you get to the other side, do you have a life review?"

"Yes."

"How does that work?"

"In a very loving way. I could see the things I did and did not do, but it was all for the learning experience."

"Have you learned from it, Sam?"

"Yes."
"Did you learn what not to do and what to do?"
"I learned what I did."
"That maybe you were unaware of?"
"Yes, my choices. I looked at my choices."
"Do you want to return sometime or do you want to stay there?"
"God is so omnipotent. God is so beautiful. I would never want to leave and yet, sometimes, I do feel that I would like to have voice, hands and feet again."
"What sort of body do you have?"
"It is spirit."
"What is your purpose there?"
"I enjoy helping these women, or the one, Sue. I enjoy assisting her in helping others go to the light of God and to be with the angels. That is my purpose. I stand at the edge and cheer them on!"
"Is it ALL about God?"
"What do you mean?"
"Do we live just to see God? What is our purpose?"
"Our purpose is to grow the light inside, in the creation of the perfection that we are, created by Creator. To grow, to come to the Earth, and live as human beings – to evolve and continue evolving – to be all that we can be both on Earth and here."
"Does God experience life through us? Does God experience what we experience?"

"I would not put it that way – no."
"But everything is here for us to experience?"
"Yes."
"Do you get to choose how you are going to come back?"
"It has already been determined."
"Did you have a voice in that?"
"Absolutely."
"Would you like to share anything else with us at this time?"
"Inside each one of you is a beautiful being, created in perfection, waiting to be discovered. I wish you all could see what we see."
"Thank you, Sam."

"LOVE,
LOVE,
LOVE,
it cannot be
said enough"

Walk Gently

on the

Earth

Walk Gently on the Earth

One week later, through the help of Kris, I called on my sacred friends once again to ask if they would share more information with us. Emma was the first to come through.

"Hello, Emma, thank you for being present and sharing information with us. Can you explain more about the different realms?"

"Yes, there are places for us – places for the humans. There are places for those that are of a higher realm, such as angels. And there are realms in the angelic realm. There are also realms for the masters and those that are highly evolved; and we can travel with each other through these realms so we may visit each other. But there are special places every individual needs to be. It is like our own little station."

"Is that where we learn on the other side?"

"Yes, it is where we learn."

"Do we move on to different realms or do we just stay in one according to who we are?"

"We can communicate and visit. We can learn to evolve in that way."

"But we stay in our own realm?"

"We live in our own realm."

"What is the realm that you are in, Emma?"

"I'm in the realm of the humans."

"What's it like?"

"It's beautiful, oh, it's beautiful. It's all wonderful!"

"So are all humans in that realm?"

"No. There are other places for those of the dark – for those that carry dark. They stay away. They cannot come this close to the earthly plane and they cannot be in our realm. They are kept in a place until they can evolve so they can not hurt us with darkness."

"So could they potentially hurt you with darkness where you are?"

"In our human realm it is all of light and love. There is no darkness."

"So they just couldn't even exist there?"

"No. This light is so pure. It can't be tainted with any type of darkness. That is not allowed."

"Is there a place or realm for animals, Emma?"

"It is more like energy, the animal energy. They do have little spirits but it isn't like being in the human realm. They have their little energy spirits and they evolve and they come and go, but on a smaller scale."

"Do you have any animals there with you?"

"Not in the human realm."

"Can you visit the animal realm – like if you lost a dog or something?"

"Oh, yes, Sam just had one come to him."

"So they can cross over too. They can come visit you and you can go visit them?"

"Oh, yes."

"Was this a previous pet of Sam's?"

"Yes, they never met before in human life, but it was a dog that his wife and children had. They got him after Sam came here and the dog just crossed back. They have been playing. So, yes, all is in order and ALL is beautiful. There is no sadness and I wish there was no sadness there on your side."

"Yes, there is a lot of sadness here."

"Too much sadness – too much sadness in this area. In the area of my school, in the area of the kids and the people, even the teachers. It is too sad and I don't know – I wish I could help them. It is much harder than I thought it would be, to not be seen or heard but to be there. It is very difficult."

"It must be very hard. Do you feel frustration?"

"Not so much frustration, but I feel their pain and their sadness and yet I am happy and I have to be here – but I do miss them."

"Do you have anything else to share right now Emma?"

"There are some here that wish to speak. Sam is here."

"Thank you, Emma."

"Sam?"

"Yes, it is very nice to find voice once again. This is happening more often than I ever expected or dreamed. The dog, Otis, is a very happy and fun dog. I always wanted to have a dog named Otis and she, my beautiful wife, named him in honor of me after I left. We play – experiencing one more little connection of beauty and love.

"There are others here who would like to share their experience with you, one of whom is Lucy."

"What would you like to share, Lucy?" (As I began to transcribe from the tape recording I noticed that the voice of Lucy was almost a whisper and remembered during the actual channeling that it was a struggle to get her to speak up enough even to be recorded.)

"I want to thank you. I want to thank you so much for helping me. There was no way I could have left. I was stuck. I would still be stuck; I would be stuck forever. I know I frightened you when I came to you that night in your sleep. You were taken back. I tried to do it in a way not to frighten you. That's why I appeared to you sitting in a field of yellow flowers. My pain was so great. You and the healing mothers took me and helped me. I killed myself. I did it with my boyfriend. I did it to spite my mother – she hated me. And when we left, he moved on; but I stayed there. After all that pain you four encouraged me. You encouraged me with love to go and I did; and I am so grateful. You helped me so much and I am here now in this beautiful world of light, forgiven and loved unconditionally. I want to let my mother know she is forgiven and I love her even in spite of all that transpired during my life. It was a short time for me to be on Earth, but I will come back again."

"Thank you, Lucy."

The next person to come through was the very angry young girl who appeared to me on several nights in succession – the little suicide bomber. (Still sounding irritated and angry.)

"What is your name?" She was not going to give me a name but her presence was strong and clear. "Did you come to me after you had already crossed or before?"

"After – after I had crossed. After they had done that to me and I was so angry. I was *so* angry and that's why I came in. I wanted to show you – to show you what they had done to me. That's why I frightened you so much. I did not deserve this, *I did not deserve this!* I was too young and they just strapped me with those things and I was not ready to go and I did not want to go. And yet my life was worthless to them.

"I came to you in anger and tried to show you that I was blown up and that's why I was so frightening. But I want to thank you and your friends for helping me see and go. I am much better here, but I still feel I didn't deserve that. None of the suicide bombers do, even though they think that they are doing the right thing. I never thought that and I never wished to have had that done to me. But I want to thank you."

"Are you okay now?"

"Yes, I am okay."

"But you still feel sad to me."

"I'm okay."

"Are you happy?"

"I'm still learning what that is."

"Please try to be happy."

"I am much better off."

"How is it you can speak my language so well?"

"There are no limitations here. There is only universal language."

"I see."

"Salaam, salaam."

"You're welcome, little one."

Some souls that have such a traumatic experience need much time to heal at the soul level before they can move through their transition. They receive a great amount of help and assistance.

"Emma? Do you have anyone else who wishes to speak?"

"Yes, but he doesn't want his name published. He doesn't want to cause any more pain to his family. You helped him a great deal and he wants to thank you."

"How did I help him?"

"He is a friend of Heather's. He died in a car accident as a teenager."

I instantly knew who this was. He was a very bright soul and still spoke with the same inquisitive inflection he had when I first met him.

"Yes, I still don't understand how you can do this. You sat there with me (in spirit through a meditative state) as I watched my own funeral. You sat with me and we watched the whole thing. I was amazed and asked 'How can you do this?' You said that it took a long time and you learned over the years. I am so sorry to have left my mom in that way and she blames herself everyday. It is not her fault. It was the way I chose to go and it was not an accident – it just happened. I am still supporting my family whom I love so much. I remember when they closed the casket, I got really upset and you just helped me. You said, "That's not you, that's just your shell." I will never forget these things and I will be eternally grateful because you helped me move on more quickly."

"So what do you do now?"

I remarked to Kris at this point that they don't seem to be able to say much about what they do.

"Maybe they're not supposed to or maybe we just can't understand it," said Kris.

"Why can't you be more specific about what you actually do over there?"

"It would take years and reams of paper."

"Do we have the capacity to understand?"

"You have the capacity to do anything. You are just like I am, only in physical form. Except on this side, we remember all–we have ALL memory.

"Universal memory?"

"Yes, yes, you could say it that way."

"The One consciousness?"

"Yes, the All That Is, the One, the consciousness with One mind. And we see our own lifetimes. We see where we have been and where we are going. We have all understanding, and yet when we come back to physical form, we only understand this physical form."

"Thank you so much for sharing with us," I said to the fine young man who was speaking.

My next question was about the method of communication we were experimenting with.

"Is the bilateral stimulation and working in the One Consciousness state to connect with Source Mind a key for us as humans in this realm? In this physical life are we to be able to understand the quantum field and expand our healing abilities on all levels?"

The answer came from Sam.

"Yes, very much so, we are evolving very quickly. We are learning to incorporate the physical and spiritual together. We now understand that the two are not completely separate as was thought in the past (that you are either dead or alive). Now we know we are eternal and can affect the body with the brain in this way to help us understand. However, it is also because the veil has become so thin between the two sides. This could never have happened a century ago."

"So as we continue to work in this state of consciousness, we are actually able to access Universal truth, Universal consciousness?"

"Yes, of course."

Addressing both Kris and me, Sam continued:

"This was not a mistake, this meeting between the two of you is right, deemed so. The two of you will help each other help others. Reaching one by one and touching the hearts of one by one is how the world will evolve. It is a time of turmoil, of difficulty. We have spent much time through many millennia, evolving with many growing pains. We are at a point where things are moving very quickly and things will change. You may ask how? How can we change the hearts and minds of so many on one planet? It can be done. It is being done right now, this moment, between the heart connection of you both and others all over the world. Just be."

"Is there more to share with us?"

"Yes, very much so. This time the answer came from Light Beings and Masters collectively. "There are many with this Universal awareness already and you are yet another avenue to prove that our two worlds are melting together. The vibration makes this possible. There is great hope that both realms, human and spirit, will be able to co-exist. This will bring about a new kind of happiness and security, making grief more bearable and giving people a new perspective. This new outlook will provide new ways of thinking because the threat of death, separation, and loneliness will no longer exist.

Information is coming through quickly now. DNA, cellular memory, vibration, and quantum physics can be accessed to heal the mind and body at lightening speed. At the same time the Earth vibration needs to be raised in consciousness to heal the planet.

"Walk gently on the Earth. She is choking and is in pain with too many pollutants and toxins. She needs cleansing, her waters need to be purified, her air needs to once again be clear, and her ground purged. We are connecting to help this come about. All the realms are uniting dear ones.

"War is an ancient, outdated technique in today's world. The human race has evolved to a point of not needing to overpower one another. Our minds and very thoughts are able to tap into Source and create our reality. Wouldn't it be wonderful to live in your very highest potential without the angst of pain and worry?

"This can be done and created on a global scale. Each race has the opportunity to look inwardly and find Source, no matter what they name the Creator."

"The possibilities are endless. There is much talk right now of manifestation. This concept, when used globally, will heal and change the world. It has taken all this time for the human race to come to a point of understanding.

"These words are the Masterly information which many enlightened ones worked very diligently to achieve. This is the way of healing miracles and manifesting.

"We, the ones in the Light, are very excited to share this concept with you as you are now ready and capable to understand and achieve it. Help us help you! Much will change very quickly in the near future. Open your hearts to it. Open your minds to it."

"Follow the message of the young girl, Emma."

"I am not dead, I am alive!

"LOVE, LOVE, LOVE – it cannot be said enough."

"Yes, Emma agreed to bring about her message in this way. So have others who were traumatically involved in recent events. Are you learning from these events or merely walking through them, carrying the grief and pain? Can you actually change the mass-consciousness enough to stop the trauma from occurring on the entire planet?

"We are here to say YES! YOU CAN!

"Every thought, every action, will manifest in whatever way it has been formulated."

"This powerful concept has been shared with us for a long time now. Have you ever realized the serious responsibility that comes with your thoughts and actions? Each of us is completely responsible for every thought and action in our lives – no one else.

"Next time something comes up and you can't understand why you feel blocked or stuck, look at your past thoughts surrounding the situation. Did you perhaps think "I'll never be able to do that," your past thought pattern created the reality you are currently experiencing. You can break through that barrier by choosing your thoughts and actions carefully."

"How does negativity serve you? Do we really need to hang on to jealousy, anger, vindictiveness, greed and judgment? These things actually hurt us more than we fully understand by manifesting as disease, ill health and unhappiness.

"Follow your dreams. Follow your heart. There is a new awakening occurring, even now. We carry all the information for perfect health in each cell of the body. We carry information about past generations and past lives in our DNA. The human body, mind, and spirit is a miraculous design. The human race is evolving rapidly."

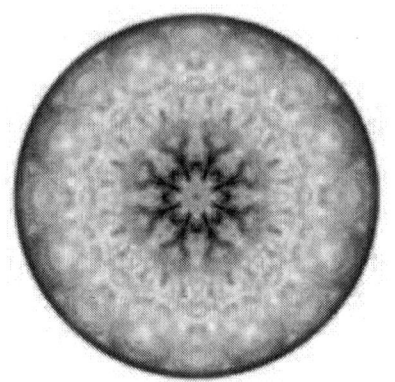

Our Endless Life

Our Endless Life

We are connected by a thread of consciousness. We do not live solitary lives. We are spiritual beings in physical bodies in a physical world. There is a purpose to our lives. It is connecting with each other in relationships without conditions. It is experiencing uninhibited love for family, friends, creatures, and nature. It is liberating.

Our obligation is not only to ourselves but to each other, the animals, and the earth. Kindness balances our life and the world around us. Our obligation is to lift into our higher state of being. Grace opens us, frees us of judgments, and dissolves our grudges. The time has come to embrace our greater nature. It is who we truly are.

When we become conscious that we are spirit, our heart opens and we are filled with an inner strength. Grief and pain no longer weigh us down.

As I sat outside, in my sacred place under the large, old Ponderosa pine tree, the following information was shared with me from my guides, angels and masters of Spirit. On several occasions, through meditation – the Masters, speaking in terms of collective consciousness, spirit and humans as one, guided me, with pen in hand, to record these words:

"In the beginning, men and women walked the earth as complete equals, complementing all things. Humans fell away from contact with us and evolved into an ego mind-set. There was love and beauty in the world, but everyone wanted their beliefs and needs to be the only ones.

We lost our connection and began to remember only our current life. We concerned ourselves with earthly matters more than connecting with the light of higher consciousness. The memory of our divine origin escaped us.

We as souls have existed for millennia – many, many lives. As a human, all we can do is learn to make choices as graciously and wisely as we know how in that moment. Life is like a play in which we are actors, interwoven in the Divine Light. One choice leads us in one direction, another in a different direction. One choice may bring us a positive experience, another a negative one. But they are both our choices. We have a choice in every matter and any choice is acceptable for our spiritual growth (although certain choices do bring us greater tranquility). We may choose difficult paths, or not, and achieve the same end. We learn to let ourselves and others make "mistakes." We learn to give and receive mercy. Choices and decisions teach us how to live for today, in *this* moment, in *this* hour. Focusing on yesterday is living in an old state of mind – no longer who we are. Focusing on tomorrow (beyond building a blueprint to fulfill the highest and best in us) is living in a state of mind that forgets we already are a divine good self.

All experiences are part of the grand vision of our creative spirit. In play and loving come moments of genuine holiness, filling us to capacity. There are no mistakes in our choices. It is only in the human form that we judge ourselves and others. Through life and life again (and again), we *remember* not to judge ourselves and, thus, we learn not to judge others.

We are responsible for our choices, however, because all actions have consequences. Actions made in fear lead to chaos. Being mindful and always present in goodwill creates peace. Our attitudes and behaviors affect others in ways we may never know, positive or negative, because we are all part of a collective consciousness – the *pool* of the mind of Source.

Is there a master plan for our lives? Before we are born, we have a plan yet we may spend life trying to find our purpose, never figuring it out. This is acceptable because there is no judgment. All That Is does not judge us; we are only loved.

The Source of all things does not favor one religion as more correct than another. Doctrines resulted from human interpretation, handed down through generations. Many holy books contain self-serving information founded in human emotion. Some information was lost, some purposely excluded. Many religions teach heaven and hell. We are here to tell you that only love and peace are on the other side of the Great Divide.

In our spirit nature, we understand why we are physical beings and why our life is the way it is, why we do what we do. It is because we learn from everything we do. We can live life the gentle way, or the tough way. Either way, we learn. We learn the necessity of goodness, compassion and resourcefulness. We learn how to enjoy the splendor of life in all of its forms. We learn to strive for what is best in us and share the wisdom of insights already in our spirit. Why? So others may also be kindled in the vision of their inner self. The purpose of life is to share blessedness – a light into all the dark corners. Accepting ourselves and others as we are (in the moment) takes us to a new plateau in our life experiences, grows us larger in our heart and mind, healing our pain, sadness, and despair.

When present in our whole being, we are fully *awake*, no longer asleep and no longer wandering absently through life without direction. We are living in our authenticity as we have been created to be.

How do we live the spiritual life? How do we become our full self now? We learn to forgive.

How do we find mercy in this world filled with chaos? It is easier to love all of humanity as a whole than those who cause us grief. Yet, to find peace in ourselves, it is necessary. When we stop blaming others for merely being human, our heart becomes lighter and our mind is free. Forgiveness is not of the action. Forgiveness is not withholding justice. But in our heart we see a soul striving; we see another lost.

How do we find balance in our emotions when harm and violence are all around us? We find a still place within. In meditation we are able to feel compassion and to perceive the larger picture. We may not comprehend why terrible things happen and we may not abide cruel behaviors, but, with inner stillness, we can sense the desperation that drives a person and can appreciate the human struggle. With inner stillness we are able to see a soul seeking survival and a way to the light. Forgiveness does not exonerate injustice and does not overlook crime. Forgiveness is letting go of our resentment so our heart lightens and we are free of the disharmony that keeps us from moving forward in our lives.

Lingering within the divine resonance, we feel the strands of life in all the realms. We feel the angels' presence, their light of insight filling and expanding us. It is the love of Source we breathe in, releasing all that is not still. Humanity is coming closer and closer to this light. All upon the earth are rising. We are embarking upon a time of great spiritual understanding. Mother Earth will once again be what she was created to be.

You each have a beautiful spirit inside of you wanting to get out in order to be who you truly are. We are here to show you how to see yourselves as we do. Many are working very hard to help you.

The vibration of earth has been dense, slow and heavy. Now the vibration is faster and lighter. Self-awareness and the desire to be of service are increasing. Despite our fears and doubts, no matter how bad things look, the human race *is* maturing. We will come to treat the earth and the animals with respect. We will come to see each other as brothers and sisters.

The Great Bear, the Gray Wolf, the Coyote, the White Buffalo and the Golden Eagle wish for you to know it is time to help them regain the quality of life they once enjoyed on this planet. They have feeling, emotion, and communication skills that humankind used to be aware of long ago. It is likened to human telepathy. There will be a time again when humans will be able to communicate with each other in this way and also with the animals and plants of this Earth.

The equality of men and women and all creatures will change. It was not the intention of Source Mind to create male dominance in the world; men created this by removing some truths in the sacred writing. Spirit did not intend for one gender to be more powerful than the other. Rendering women subservient to men put the world out of balance, affecting all of life on earth.

There is a fine line between the human and spiritual sides of life. Both sides are experienced during sleep – some people remember this as dreams. In sleep the essential self departs the physical body and explores the universe.

A new world is evolving. Many people are awakening to higher consciousness, seeing beyond their humanness and understanding we are all connected. War is based on fear. We all are shifting into a new state of mind. Unite and it will be gentler. Be not afraid. Come closer. We are with you.

Dear Ones, we are preparing the world to once again be the glorious place it was when every being looked upon each other as light – when animals, insects, plants, trees and minerals were all respected. Humankind has drifted. We have come to help you. You are magnificent beings formed in the light of All That Is. You have just lost your way. We are here – angels, guides and masters – reaching out to you. Dear Ones, it is time."

As I learned when I briefly died during surgery, outside the physical body we are *still alive*. We do not die. At physical death we merely lose the dense physical body. We simply lose the shell within which we have walked and awaken to our light body. Death is merely a transition to our eternal form. We are the same person, only free of pain and sadness, standing in our light of perfection.

My journeys through time and other worlds have shown me that life is an opportunity to be our full Self. Our inherent spiritual nature is light and there is no darkness when we turn ourselves ON. How do we do that? We reach beyond ourselves and help others who suffer more greatly. Living in our goodness heals our heart, unburdens our mind, and frees us of our self judgments. Serenity becomes our song. We let go of regret and fear.

My experience visiting the masters, assisting souls to the light and remembering treacheries of one people against another, along with the deep loyalties of my friends and family and the music that pours through me, all quiet my heart and still my mind. In the stillness I find fulfilling life. In the stillness we hear the angel's song and live in the angel's light.

Sue Scudder

"It is all so simple," says the Divine.

"Love yourselves as I have loved you."

"Be love, create love, and love all things."

Epilogue

This is a true story. This book is my experience. May this writing, inspired from my life and soul memories, touch you with divine fulfillment from the spark of life within us all.

I continue my commitment to serve Mother Earth and humanity. During my life adventures I have learned many things. I am especially excited to have discovered new modalities of healing to help others.

As time continues to heal our community many outstanding events and opportunities, initiated by Emma's loved ones, are emerging in honor of Emma. She gave them a voice. Kindness and altruism replaces the sadness.

I feel profoundly humbled and blessed to have had each and every experience in my life. The people who have graced my path are a special gift. I thank all of them and look forward to many new adventures.

It amazes me to watch life's events unfold – one connecting to another, weaving an intricate web of perfect design. It is easy to see the connection of all things. It is already beginning, reaching out from one hand to another in love.

The experiences in my life have given me a heightened commitment to serve others on both sides.

The music still flows through me, providing a sense of peace and serenity. May you carry that peace with you as you walk in a good way. . . .

Namaste

Sue Scudder

"We must learn to love. We must learn to be kind. We must learn to live in that way. We can do this by each person living and being in that kindness and honoring each other: honoring each other with the respect we all deserve, no matter where we are in life, no matter what walk of life we have."

Emma

Glossary

All That Is - a phrase that refers to the wholeness of life, especially to the spirit that lives in all things.

Angels - The word angel means messenger. Angels bridge our physical reality with their pure spiritual energy that embodies God's perfect love for us. They bridge heaven to earth and create openings - like doorways - to the divine within you.

Automatic Writing - The ability to write intelligible messages in an altered state without conscious control or knowledge of what is being written.

Channel - The medium through which a spirit guide purportedly communicates with the physical world; to serve as a medium for a spirit guide.

Channeling - Transmitting of messages from one world to another.

Contact - Connection with someone else on this or another plane of existence.

Council of Twelve - A group of nonphysical Ascended Masters in the spiritual hierarchy working with humanity and the Earth to help facilitate the great shift in consciousness. The Council of Twelve is a rotating group of light beings including Jesus, Mother Mary, Lord Kuthumi, Saint Germain, Paramahansa Yogananda, Quan Yin and more.

Creator - The Source, God, the supreme intelligence that created Totality, is the essence of Totality, and is the law sustaining it (Universal Law); one main principal behind all there is and everything being a part of that one main principle.

Death - Afterlife, life on the other side - discarnate realm of existence.

Dense body - The physical body.

Discarnate - Without body. One who survived death, and now exists in the etheric realm in astral body

Divine Light - Celestial radiance perceived by the Third Eye; eternal brilliance within all beings, brighter than the Sun, realized by turning away from the physical senses and looking within and whose mystical union confers truth, consciousness, and bliss.

Earth plane - State of incarnation on Earth. Material existence.

EMDR - Eye movement desensitization and reprocessing (EMDR) is a form of psychotherapy that was developed to resolve symptoms resulting from disturbing and unresolved life experiences. It uses a structured approach to address past, present, and future aspects of disturbing memories. The approach was developed by Francine Shapiro to resolve the development of trauma-related disorders resulting from exposure to traumatic or distressing events.

Energy - Life force, cosmic ether, healing medium, vitalizing force, cosmic electricity. Electromagnetic fields consisting of positive, negative, and neutral charges which build and sustain the human body and all other matter.

Ethereal - Of the intangible celestial spheres; the non-physical space of universe; heavenly; spiritual in nature.

God - 1. *(Judeo-Christianity)* Creator and sustainer of the universe. 2. *(Theosophy)* Transcendent being who guides and controls the course of planetary evolution. 3. Sum total of all that is. 4. *(Islam)* Lord of the universe who cannot be represented by any form. 5. *(Hinduism)* The One who plays the game of life by becoming the Many, losing itself in the creation and finding its way back to unity; supreme being, personal friend, teacher, and lover who knows the heart of all beings. 6. *(mysticism)* Indwelling spirit within all beings; one's highest self realized through contemplation or service; eternal, infinite, all-wise, all-knowing, all-loving, ever-free radiant presence. 7. *(Humanism)* Impersonal spirit of selfless love. 8. All That Is.

Guided imagery - A program of directed thoughts and suggestions that guide your imagination toward a relaxed focused state of meditation.

Great Spirit - The Divine spirit that moves and lives within all things.

Medicine Wheel - A medicine wheel is a Native American sacred circle that represents the Universe and the balance of all creation. It is often symbolized in art around a home, or an actual medicine wheel is created on the ground in ritual or ceremony. The medicine wheel is used by Native American spiritual practices, and has also been adopted by the metaphysical movement.

Out of Body/Astral Projection – (or astral travel) is an esoteric interpretation of any form of out-of-body experience that assumes the existence of an astral body separate from the physical body and capable of traveling outside it. Astral projection or travel denotes the astral body leaving the physical body to travel in the astral plane.

Past Lives - Reincarnation, literally "to be made flesh again", is the belief that the soul, after death of the body, comes back to earth in another body. According to one belief, a new personality is developed during each life in the physical world, but the soul remains constant throughout the successive lives.

Portal - The entryway between realms.

Soul Contracts - Before we come to Earth in any lifetime we choose all that is around us and all that we came here to experience and accomplish. In some theories this is done at the time of our creation. A Sacred or Soul Contract is an agreement the soul makes before birth.

We promise to do certain things for ourselves, for others, and for divine purposes.

Teepee Ring - Stones were placed around the bottom of the teepee cover to hold the teepee in place. Several inches of the cover overlapped on the ground. Over time even when the stones disappear the rings are still imbedded in the ground.

Telepathic Communication - The psychic phenomena by which communication occurs between minds, or mind-to-mind communication. Such communication includes thoughts, ideas, feelings, sensations and mental images.

The One Consciousness – If a group of human beings align their consciousness (in their highest state of being) on any one thing; be it healing, manifesting, love, peace etc. it can automatically shift the consciousness of all humankind.

Vortex – In Sedona vortexes are created, not by wind or water, but from spiraling spiritual energy. The vortexes of Sedona are named because they are believed to be spiritual locations where the energy is right to facilitate prayer, mediation and healing.

About the Author

Sue Scudder is an internationally recognized musician, healing arts practitioner, author, and educator. She incorporates over two decades of expertise utilizing several modalities in the healing arts field, and is dedicated to evolving human consciousness. Sue's mission is to promote and facilitate healing by empowering others to transform those aspects of self that are limiting, enabling them to live life in their highest potential.

Sue is committed to continue her clairvoyant work in service to the collective consciousness of All.

A thirty-year veteran in the music field as a teacher and gifted composer, Sue's passion is to share her healing, ambient musical improvisations with the world.

For more information about Sue's practice, *Three Sisters Holistic Health,* or her music, visit: SueScudder.com

"Music has the ability to touch us in ways nothing else can. So is the same for Spirit energy, which is an innate potential inside each one of us."

Sue Scudder

Author's Note

I hope this story of personal stillness — providing peaceful glimpses into the spirit world, afterlife, souls in transition, past-life memory, and the angelic realm — invites you to reflect on your own spiritual journey.

Other works by Sue Scudder

Global Theta™ Meditation; one mind . . . one purpose . . . World Peace* CD © *2007

This inspired meditation CD takes you to the theta brainwave state of manifestation and focuses on peaceful existence and a unified purpose toward world harmony. Collaborated with Donna Aazura. Released February, 2008

Sacred Friends CD © 2005

Created in celebration of the Earth, its people and the mystery of realms beyond, this CD features soothing, melodic sounds of piano accompanied by flute, strings and light percussion.

Stand in the Light Meditation CD © 2002

In collaboration with Karen Jolly, known for her extraordinary expressions in meditation, discover love, truth and infinite wisdom within. Guided vocal meditation with piano accompaniment.

Celebration of Light CD © 2001

Inspired performances on piano accompanied by flute and strings are a musical interpretation of nature. "Seek joy in the simple beauty nature has to share."

Wildflowers, Nature's Inspirations © 1994

Sue Scudder

About The Artist

Cover and Art Design: Artist/photographer Sophia Rose

Sophia Rose incorporates a deep sense of spirituality into all of her art, whether it is photography, painting or what ever she happens to be creating in the moment.

She combines her love for nature, meditation and photography into creating her kaleidoscopic mandalas. While making these meditation masterpieces, she calls in the energies of the plants, animals or crystals she is working with and requests that they encode their wisdom into the images.

A mandala is a geometric pattern, typically circular or square, that symbolically represents the cosmos and is used for meditation purposes. The mandala originated in the Hindu religion, in which it was first used as a design element in temples.

The unique nature mandalas that Sophia creates capture the essence of the energies she works with. As a result intricate patterns and images appear within the design itself.

The Voice Across the Veil

We invite you to spend some time gazing at these mandalas to find your own perceptions of the images within.

Others find her work to be healing, uplifting and inspirational. Sophia finds great joy and purpose through her creative work.

List of original subjects used in Sophia's kaleidoscopic mandalas:

Cover design – Blue Pansie

Chapter 1 –   Assorted flowers in honor of Sophia's grandmother.
Chapter 2 –   Azurite Crystal
Chapter 3 –   Pink Rose
Chapter 4 –   Dahlia flowers
Chapter 5 –   Tourmaline Crystals
Chapter 6 –   Roses
Chapter 7 –   Rose
Chapter 8 –   Peony flower
Chapter 9 –   Bromeliad

End of Part One: Blue Pansie

Chapter 10 – Flower bouquet in honor of Sophia's grandmother
Chapter 11 – Amethyst Crystal
Chapter 12 – Dog fur: image from Sophia's pet Standard Poodle
Chapter 13 – Rose
Chapter 14 – Azurite Crystal

End – Blue Pansie

It is a joy to share my continuing journey. More often than not as I describe my experiences, others open to sharing their personal stories about communicating with loved ones and the unseen world. I would be grateful if you would share your insights and stories with me.

Please contact me at:
Sue Scudder
P.O. Box 253
Pine, CO 80470

You can send me a message or tell me your story at:
SpeakingWithTheSpirits.com

Sue Scudder

The Voice Across the Veil

If you found this book helpful, please take the time to leave a review so that future readers of this book can use your feedback to make a meaningful decision for themselves. Thank you.

ISBN: 1530283353

Made in the USA
Columbia, SC
10 March 2018